CW00764919

Trials and Tribulations

*Uncommon Tales
of the
Common Law*

JAMES WILSON

WS
&H

Wildy, Simmonds & Hill Publishing

First published in Great Britain 2015 by Wildy, Simmonds & Hill Publishing

Website: www.wildy.com

Wilson, James
Trials and Tribulations

ISBN 9780854901715
Printed and bound in Great Britain

To Sam and Aran

Contents

Acknowledgements

A number of the essays in this book appeared originally as articles in the *New Law Journal* and *Criminal Law & Justice Weekly*. My thanks to the respective editors, Jan Miller and Diana Rose, and their editorial teams, is extended accordingly.

As usual I was able to call upon family help: my brother John Wilson read through several drafts of the book, offering suggestions going well beyond merely identifying spelling mistakes and solecisms. My sister Annette Harris and her husband Neil also read several parts and made a number of comments and corrections.

Several of my colleagues past and present joined as unpaid editors and subeditors at different times. Helen Sheridan kindly read through the entire draft. Individual chapters were read by Toby Frost, Judy John and Sally Thomas. Of course, responsibility for any remaining errors is mine alone.

I am very grateful to Anne-Marie Forker (www.forkerfotos. com) for the cover photograph, not simply for taking the picture but for her artistic ideas as well.

Thanks are due as well to Andrew Riddoch and the rest of the team at Wildy, Simmonds & Hill, for their always professional support and for their management of the project.

Most important remains my family for their support throughout, so the greatest thanks go to Mona, Sam and Aran. Mona donned her metaphorical surgical mask as Dr Mona Wilson BDS by casting an expert eye over the medico-legal section, while Sam and Aran helped with checking the running order and with various other aspects of production.

Preface

The acclaimed novelist Ian McEwan once said about common law judgments:[1]

> It was the prose that struck me first. Clean, precise, delicious. Serious, of course, compassionate at points, but lurking within its intelligence was something like humour, or wit, derived perhaps from its godly distance, which in turn reminded me of a novelist's omniscience. I continued to note the parallels between our professions, for these judgments were like short stories, or novellas; the background to some dispute or dilemma crisply summarised, characters drawn with quick strokes, the story distributed across several points of view and, towards its end, some sympathy extended towards those whom, ultimately, the narrative would not favour.

This is the second book of short essays on law stories that I have written.[2] It has the same intention as the first – a look at a broad range of cases or other legal dilemmas that have caught my interest over the years. Some of the cases contained interesting facts that are strange, tragic, comic or bittersweet. Others contained challenging moral, ethical and philosophical dilemmas. The best involved all of the above, along with the incidental pleasure of well-crafted prose, as described by McEwan.

With nearly a thousand years of the common law to choose from, there was no shortage of material. Most of the cases were drawn from England and Wales but I did not confine myself

---

[1] Ian McEwan, 'The law versus religious belief', *Guardian*, 5 September 2014.
http://www.theguardian.com/books/2014/sep/05/ian-mcewan-law-versus-religious-belief. Retrieved 9 September 2014.
[2] The first is *Cases Causes and Controversies: fifty tales from the law* (Wildy, Simmonds & Hill, 2012). For simplicity I shall refer to it hereafter simply as *Cases, Causes and Controversies*. Likewise I shall refer to my second book, *Court and Bowled: tales of cricket and the law* (Wildy, Simmonds & Hill, 2014) simply as *Court and Bowled*. Two other books in which I had some involvement were *Cases that Changed Our Lives* (LexisNexis, 2010) and *Cases that Changed Our Lives, vol II* (LexisNexis, 2014). I wrote chapter introductions for both and was co-editor of the latter. Hereafter I will refer to both by the titles only.

to that jurisdiction, meaning the well of potential material was deeper still.

I was fortunate to receive some intelligent and constructive feedback on my first book. Partly in response I have included in this book three cases which legally trained commentators felt ought to be there even if I was not trying to write a textbook. These were *Carlill v Carbolic Smokeball*, *Donoghue v Stevenson* and *Liversidge v Anderson*. It was difficult to know where to begin with them because they are so well known. I have therefore confined myself to a short sketch of the facts of each case – enough to convey the essence to a lay reader – and then a few reflections on competing arguments. Each has some interesting points of trivia which will hopefully liven up the walk down well-trodden corridors.

The balance of the book is composed of cases and stories chosen because they reflected my own interests of human rights, constitutional law, legal history, military history and random episodes of human drama. I have organised the different essays into sections on thematic lines (with no claim to irreducible logic for the choices) and have written a short introduction to each section. The result is a mixture of cases from the ludicrous to the deadly serious, and from quirky stories to complex ethical, social and legal issues – just like the day-to-day business of the courts themselves.

Needless to say, there are still a number of well-known cases I have omitted this time around. I can only say by way of mitigation that no definitive list emerged from any of the straw polls I conducted concerning what were the essential or most noteworthy cases, bearing in mind the book is supposed to be an interesting read rather than a textbook. Besides, interesting cases continue to emerge on an almost weekly basis from the courts, so any attempt to be comprehensive would be doomed.

One change from some of my earlier writings is that I have added rather more footnotes this time around. These have been included, somewhat contradictorily, to make the book less, not more, like a dry legal textbook. Those who are interested in checking sources and finding further reading can look at the footnotes; those who are only interested in the stories and arguments as presented can ignore them.

As with my previous books, I have used the terminology appropriate to the time and place. Thus, English judges are referred to as Mr Justice Smith (thereafter Smith J), Lord Justice Smith (thereafter Smith LJ) and Lord Smith, depending on whether they are in the High Court, Court of Appeal or House of Lords/Supreme Court respectively. Australia calls appellate judges Smith JA, while New Zealand has long dispensed with 'Mr' before High Court judges. I have used 'plaintiff' and 'claimant' interchangeably, depending on which terminology was current in the case.[3] I trust no confusion results.

Each of the cases here caught my eye for one reason or another. I have long thought anyone interested in human nature and human affairs cannot fail to be interested in the stranger, quirkier and otherwise noteworthy stories of the common law. The next pages cover a few of my favourites; I hope readers will find them as engaging as I did.

---

[3] The use of the latter term was introduced in England by the Civil Procedure Rules 1998, for no particularly good reason. In fact it only served to muddy the waters, since the word 'claimant' is used in a variety of other contexts in England (someone applying for a social welfare benefit, for example), whereas 'plaintiff' was never used outside the legal world and was reasonably well-known in common parlance anyway. More pointless changes included replacing the foreboding word 'writ' with the lame 'claim form' and the easily understood 'third party' with the anodyne 'Pt 20 defendant'. Also, the well-known term 'Affidavit' was replaced by 'Statement of Truth' – another change without alteration. Most other jurisdictions did not follow suit with any of the changes.

The Supreme Court replaced the Appellate Committee of the House of Lords as the United Kingdom's highest domestic court early in the twenty-first century. Again, it was not an uncontroversial change.

Part I: Victoriana

Introduction

Mention of the Victorian era conjures up much rich and often contrasting imagery: Dickensian poverty alongside magnificent Gothic-revival public buildings; almost Puritanical standards of morality giving rise to accompanying standards of hypocrisy; the growth of general education but the retention of a rigid class system. Both the class system and hypocrisy are fully on display in the first case considered here, the fall of the Scottish landowner William Gordon-Cumming in what became known as the 'Tranby Croft Affair'. The story was a classic country house drama, at least as compelling – and in some respects less believable – than any storyline from *Downton Abbey* or *Upstairs Downstairs*.

The second case is arguably the best-known legal case of the era: the classic story of Mrs Carlill and the smoke ball 'cure' for influenza which she unwisely purchased. As with the Tranby Croft affair, the background facts contain an interesting cast of characters and some entertaining irony in the ultimate fate of the main protagonists. Unlike Tranby Croft, though, the case also has considerable legal significance, forming a landmark in the development of consumer law. As well as all of the advances in science and engineering, Victorian Britain was a time when much of modern commercial law was forged, which was no less important for the wealth of the nation. The nation remains in Carlill's debt accordingly.

Next are the legal travails of the great Victorian, Oscar Wilde, whose fall from society was much further and harsher than Gordon-Cumming's. Wilde brought a quixotic action against the Marquess of Queensberry, and after that failed found himself prosecuted for indecencies between males under s 11 of the Criminal Offences Act 1885. Why he brought the case against the Marquess has puzzled many ever since: his action was based on a lie and Wilde had to have known that there was a strong chance Queensberry would prove it. The consensus seems to be that he sacrificed himself to save Lord Douglas.

Although the obvious course would have been for Wilde simply to ignore Queensberry's provocation, I suspect it is more than likely that Queensberry would have stepped up his efforts until Wilde had no choice other than to respond. A showdown risking Wilde's public disgrace was therefore perhaps inevitable, and it is hard to see how it might have had a different outcome.

Wilde was prosecuted (and, for that matter, persecuted) for indecencies under the Criminal Offences Act 1885. He was by no means the only one. Later in the book we will see how the Act was used with at least as much cruelty against the war hero Alan Turing, and how it (and the resultant public attitude) formed part of the background to the trial of Liberace. Aside from those prosecuted under the Act, the total number of victims must be unknown. Thousands must have lived in fear and in denial of their true nature thanks to the threat of prosecution under the Act.

There remains an interesting question as to why the relevant provision of the 1885 Act was introduced in the first place. Famously, lesbianism was never illegal in Britain. Contrary to the myth, this was not because Queen Victoria or anyone else thought it did not exist. Instead, as spelt out by an uncomfortable Viscount in Parliament in the 1920s, it was because of fear that women might be blackmailed.[1] It was not uncommon in those more financially straitened times for adult women, including amongst the middle classes, to share rooms, and the Viscount clearly had in mind some below-stairs types being able to level false allegations.

But why was male conduct criminalised? The Victorians certainly thought it immoral, but they were also aware of the distinction between law and morality and did not seek to outlaw everything of which they disapproved (just as well in those more rigid times). Individualistic and laissez-faire theories were strong currents in the political and philosophical thought of the

---

[1] See Karon Monaghan QC, 'There's Nowt So Queer as Folk', in *Cases that Changed Our Lives*, vol II.

day. One would therefore have expected at least a debate before introducing a new form of criminal offence. Yet there seems to have been none. The bill which became the 1885 Act was brought in to raise the age of consent for heterosexual sex from 13 to 16, because of concerns around child prostitution. The amendment criminalising homosexual acts was brought in at the last minute by the back-bencher Henry Labouchere MP, and seems to have gone through on the nod.

At least as badly persecuted as Oscar Wilde, though for different reasons, was Captain Dreyfus, the victim of one of France's most famous injustices and the subject of the final case considered in this part. As with Wilde, bigotry of ages past was a contributing factor: in Dreyfus's case, the fact he was Jewish seems to have been the reason he was blamed for leaking intelligence to the Germans. At least, unlike Wilde, Dreyfus was rehabilitated in his own lifetime, even if there was not an entirely happy ending, as we will see.

A Royal Flush

The world of scandal and intrigue in the English country house has long provided fodder for both fiction and non-fiction writers, as reflected by Sunday evening television schedules for many years. Arguably the greatest real life saga was the Royal Baccarat Scandal of the 1890s, often called the 'Tranby Croft Affair' after the stately home where the scandal took place.

The *dramatis personae* included the then-Prince of Wales. As with his present-day counterpart, the future Edward VII had to wait many decades before becoming King, thanks to the longevity of his mother. Unlike Charles, though, one of Edward's favourite pastimes was gambling on cards, despite (or maybe because of) his mother's disapprobation and the fact that it was illegal.

The chief protagonist was not the Prince, but rather the Flashmanesque[1] Lt-Col Sir William Gordon-Cumming. Gordon-Cumming was known as a fearless hero of the colonial wars in Africa, a fearless hunter of tigers in India, and an equally fearless hunter of young wives back in Britain. He was the owner of three large if fairly unremunerative Scottish estates at the time of the scandal. According to the *Dictionary of National Biography* he revelled in the title of 'the most arrogant man in London'.

In September 1890 both the Prince and Gordon-Cumming were invited to a weekend at Tranby Croft, near Hull. At the time the house was the seat of the wealthy shipbuilder Sir Arthur Wilson, who as a member of the relatively new money set must have thought his guest list something of a coup.

The weekend's activities consisted of country pursuits during the day followed by card games in the evening. Over the course of two nights, first Sir Arthur's son and then three others whom

[1] George McDonald Fraser's classic fictional Victorian anti-hero Flashman claimed to have been present at the affair, as recorded in *Flashman and the Tiger*. He too notes the similarities between himself and Gordon-Cumming, though he finds them a source of resentment, given that Gordon-Cumming is younger and a much more authentic military hero. I won't spoil the ending, but Flashman comes up with a new explanation as to what took place and why.

he had alerted formed the view that Gordon-Cumming was cheating by altering his bets after the cards had been dealt. After consulting two other guests (an officer in Gordon-Cumming's regiment and the Master of Buckhounds (a now sadly defunct office)) they felt compelled to inform the Prince and confront Gordon-Cumming.

For Gordon-Cumming such allegations, if proven, would constitute social ruin. For the Prince any form of scandal would be almost as bad, especially since he had been somewhat notorious in his youth for adulterous affairs to rival those of Gordon-Cumming (his conquests allegedly including Alice Keppel, the great-grandmother of Camilla Parker-Bowles). One such tryst had landed him in court before, giving evidence in a divorce case.

Gordon-Cumming protested his innocence, but his accusers also faced a loss of face if they withdrew or failed to prove the allegations, never mind the fact that they had all been taking part in an illegal activity. To try and save collective face all concerned roughed out an agreement whereby Gordon-Cumming would sign a 'confession' in return for everyone else's silence.

Inevitably the secret did not stay secret for long, and multiple rumours about the scandal began to spread throughout society. Many thought the initial leak came from yet another of the Prince of Wales' mistresses, Lady Brooke, whose reputation for gossip earned her the sobriquet 'Babbling Brooke'.[2]

Gordon-Cumming's only option was a libel suit, unless his accusers backed down. They refused, and so Gordon-Cumming issued proceedings in the High Court. By dint of being a fellow Army officer of Gordon-Cumming, the Prince of Wales was compelled to give evidence. His presence ensured the trial became one of the great scandals of its day.

The case had a legal cast just as interesting as that of the card game. The trial was presided over by the Lord Chief Justice,

---

[2]   An interesting character herself, Lady Brooke was the inspiration for the song *Daisy Bell (Bicycle Built for Two)* and led quite an extraordinary life. See Suishila Anand, *Daisy: The life and loves of the Countess of Warwick* (Piatkus, 2009).

Lord Coleridge, whose career had included hearing the case of the cannibals and the cabin boy.[3] After Gordon-Cumming's case he would go on to hear Oscar Wilde's ill-fated libel action against the Marquess of Queensberry, which we consider in the next chapter. Appearing for the plaintiff was Sir Edward Clarke KC, who would also appear in Wilde's libel action. The defendants were represented by the future Lord Russell and the future Prime Minister Herbert Asquith.

Gordon-Cumming's testimony in court bore the fortitude of a cornered soldier, but ultimately he faced two insurmountable obstacles in the form of the signed confession and the fact that the Prince of Wales's testimony favoured the defendants. The jury took just 13 minutes to reject the case, leaving Gordon-Cumming's career in high society in tatters. He was dismissed from the army immediately but almost simultaneously married his wealthy American fiancée, Florence Garner, who had stood by him despite the scandal. He lived on for many years before dying an embittered man in somewhat reduced circumstances, still protesting his innocence.

The affair was later examined in detail by some distinguished lawyers, including the former Attorney-General,[4] who concluded that a miscarriage of justice had occurred. They pointed out that the accusers could never get their story straight, that Lord Coleridge's conduct of the trial was incompetent, and that Gordon-Cumming had had no reason to cheat since he did not need the money.

I find the first two reasons reasonably compelling but not, with respect, the third, which misses one crucial point: a gambler does not need a reason to cheat. Addictive gamblers seek the high of the moment and will try to win at virtually any cost.

---

[3] *R v Dudley and Stephens*. See *Cases, Causes and Controversies*, Chapter 3.
[4] See Havers et al, *The Royal Baccarat Scandal* (Souvenir Press Ltd, 1988). The first port of call for anyone wanting to learn more about the case should be W. Teignmouth Shore, *The Baccarat Case* (Obscure Press, 2006), which contains a full transcript of the trial. It was originally published in 1933 as part of the *Notable British Trials Series*.

Putting the case at its highest in his favour, therefore, one could say Gordon-Cumming did not have a fair trial – meaning that, as with all the best dramas, the truth will always remain elusive.[5]

Afterword

The Prince of Wales ensured Gordon-Cumming remained a pariah amongst the great and the good following the case, and thereby consigned him to socialise (if at all) with the middle classes everyone knew he despised. As I mentioned, Gordon-Cumming's fall was not limited to the social sphere either: in the early 1900s he and Florence were forced to relocate to a smaller house in Devon, getting by with a mere eight servants. The one thing that apparently remained constant was his infidelity, which ultimately drove Florence to drink. He died in 1930 at the age of eighty, still protesting his innocence. At the time of writing, his family still retained ownership of one of the Scottish estates, Altyre. Its website[6] sketched out the family history, though all it said about Sir William was that he 'led a colourful life in London society'.

Most extant country houses nowadays are in the hands of the National Trust or English Heritage, or the odd foreign magnate, or have been converted to hotels or schools (Tranby Croft itself is now Hull Collegiate School while one of Gordon-Cumming's houses was sold after his death and was turned into the famous public school Gordonstoun, later attended by among others the present Prince of Wales). There seems, therefore, not to be much left of the world Gordon-Cumming once inhabited. Having said that, when I was first drafting this article, an item appeared in the *Daily Mail*[7] about an apparent 'star player' at an exclusive golf club who had been accused of cheating. As the newspaper reported, he faced social ruin, his accusers faced the libel courts and the club faced unwanted media attention. So perhaps I should say *plus ça change*.

---

[5] Published in *the New Law Journal*, vol 163, 18 January 2013, p 46.
[6] http://www.altyre-estate.co.uk. (Retrieved 4 January 2013).
[7] 2 December 2012.

The Quixotic Artist

'A thump, and a murmur of voices —
("Oh why must they make such a din?")
As the door of the bedroom swung open
And TWO PLAIN CLOTHES POLICEMEN came in:

"Mr. Woilde, we 'ave come for tew take yew
Where felons and criminals dwell:
We must ask yew tew leave with us quoietly
For this is the Cadogan Hotel."

He rose, and he put down The Yellow Book.
He staggered — and, terrible-eyed,
He brushed past the plants on the staircase
And was helped to a hansom outside.'

The Arrest of Oscar Wilde at the Cadogan Hotel (1937)
John Betjeman

There are few better known Victorians than Oscar Wilde. There are also few better known Victorian court cases than Wilde's disastrous libel action and consequent criminal prosecutions, which stand as a grim reminder of the injustice meted out by prejudice past.

The origins of Wilde's legal travails are well known. He had a relationship with Lord Alfred 'Bosie' Douglas, younger son of the Marquess of Queensberry (of boxing rules fame).[8] To say Queensberry disapproved of the relationship would be an understatement, although he had been charmed by Wilde during one of their early meetings. It has been rumoured that Queensberry's eldest son had an affair with Lord Rosebery, also to Queensberry's fury, though if so there was little he could do since Rosebery was too big a fish. Instead, Queensberry resolved to finish Wilde and Bosie's relationship.

---

[8] One finds variations on the spelling of both 'Marquess' and 'Queensberry'. I have chosen what seem to be the most common, though I note that on Queensberry's own calling card he used 'Marquis'.

Polite discourse was not Queensberry's preferred mode of attack. Instead, he tried various means including turning up at one of Wilde's plays with some rotten vegetables he intended to throw at the stage. On that occasion he was thwarted by the police. Then, he left the infamous calling card at Wilde's club addressed to 'Oscar Wilde – posing somdomite' (sic).

Given that homosexuality was illegal at the time, and attracted complete social opprobrium, there was no question the message on the card was libelous. Wilde could have chosen to ignore the provocation, and many of his subsequent biographers have dwelt on the question of why he did not. For what it is worth, I think Wilde feared the Marquess would keep at him and Bosie, with steadily more aggressive tactics to which they would have to respond sooner or later.[9] Whatever the reason, Wilde chose about the most confrontational response imaginable, by suing the Marquess for criminal libel.

Wilde instructed well-known solicitors and counsel, including Sir Edward Clarke KC, and assured them that there was no truth in the Marquess's inference. The Marquess hired an equally well-known barrister, Sir Edward Carson KC, who would later gain greater fame as the effective founder of the modern province of Northern Ireland. Carson and Wilde had been contemporaries at Oxford, and Wilde mused that Carson was likely to conduct the case 'with all the bitterness of an old friend'. Once the case was underway, a reporter said of the clash between the two: 'It was a duel of thrilling interest. Mr Carson's wig throws his white, thin, clever face into sharp relief. When he is angry it assumes the immovability of a death mask.'

Queensberry put forward a straightforward defence of truth. The result was that although Wilde was the plaintiff, he was effectively on trial himself, because his case depended on him refuting Queensberry's evidence about his homosexual

[9] Wilde thought Queensberry was motivated much less by caring about Bosie, and much more about picking a fight, though Queensberry has had his defenders – see for example Linda Stratmann, *The Marquess of Queensberry: Wilde's Nemesis* (Yale University Press, 2013). Perhaps after more than a century the most apposite quote is from Wilde: 'Always forgive your enemies; nothing annoys them so much'.

activities. That evidence was in the form of supposedly 'immoral' passages in Wilde's written work and, much more dangerously for Wilde, testimony from former acquaintances of Wilde including rent boys.

Wilde had no difficulty defending his written work in the witness box. He maintained, to the amusement of the gallery and the occasional annoyance of the judge, that anything risqué was the reader's inference, not his, and that he never considered literature moral or immoral, only well written or badly written.

When faced with the testimony of his alleged former partners, however, Wilde's case collapsed. Aspiring barristers would do well to study Carson's masterful cross-examination – short, incisive questions, a logical structure, and never allowing the witness a moment's respite. As witness after witness came forth with evidence of prior relations with Wilde, Wilde's legal team told him that the game was up, and the case was withdrawn.

The result was a complete victory for the Marquess and public humiliation for Wilde, but the latter's troubles were just beginning. The police were presented with ample evidence collated by Queensberry about Wilde's actions, and he was duly charged with indecency offences. He was arrested whilst drinking hock and seltzer (a popular Victorian drink, favoured by W. G. Grace among others) at the Cadogan Hotel, a scene made more famous by Betjeman's poem quoted above.

Much speculation has been made about why Wilde did not flee to France before the police arrived at the hotel, as he apparently had time to do. Some argue that he did not actually have enough time to escape, since he would never have made a ferry in time. Others maintain that he was engaging in some intellectually motivated self-flagellation, wherein he decided after years of hedonism to seek self-fulfillment by the alternative means of austerity and punishment.

Once on trial Wilde continued to deny the allegations, although he did give one of his most famous speeches in reply to a question about 'the love that dare not speak its name'. When the jury failed to reach a verdict, Wilde was released on bail. By that stage, even Sir Edward Carson was moved to argue that Wilde had suffered enough. But the prosecutors presumably felt that there had been too much publicity for them to let it go. Wilde was re-tried and finally convicted. He received the maximum sentence of two years' imprisonment, the judge snarling gratuitously – and not a little absurdly – that the sentence was wholly inadequate, and that it was 'the worst case' he had ever tried – this from a man who had presumably presided over murder trials. It serves as a vivid reminder of the social climate of the day (which may also have contributed to the prosecutorial zeal).

The stress of the trial and punishment destroyed Wilde's health as well as his reputation and finances. Two years after he was released he died, aged 46, in poverty and exile in France. In his final days he was heard to remark about his reduced surroundings that 'the wallpaper and I are fighting a battle to the death: one of us has to go'. He also said ruefully that 'like dear Francis of Assisi, I am married to poverty, except in my case the marriage is not a success'. Queensberry and the legal system had destroyed much, but evidently not his legendary wit.[10]

---

[10] Another story occasionally said to be about Wilde is that he converted to Roman Catholicism, but took a pragmatic approach: when asked on his deathbed whether he rejected the devil, he responded 'now is not the time to be making new enemies'. In fact, the quote was probably by Voltaire, and certainly not Wilde, though I imagine he would have approved of it.

Mrs Carlill and the Quack

More than a century after it was decided, the case of *Carlill v The Carbolic Smoke Ball Company*[11] remains one of the most searched-for cases out of hundreds of thousands on the large electronic legal databases. Its fame has been said to derive from 'the combination of its striking facts, the memorable name of the defendant and its product, and the number of different legal points to be derived from it.'[12] I would imagine another of the chief reasons is the imagery of the Victorian quack, and the general imagery of Victorian England which it evokes, both of which have long been a fertile source for writers and entertainers.

Often quacks are portrayed for comic effect. But in the real world of pollution, squalor, epidemics and pandemics that was life for most of the population in Victorian Britain, the sale of crank remedies had a much darker side. It is impossible to know how many innocent victims lost their livelihoods, their health or both, from purchasing various types of snake oil. For all of the legal interest and factual quirks of Carlill's case, therefore, we should remember the serious underlying fact of desperate people seeking desperate measures.

In 1895, an American inventor called Frederick Augustus Roe formed the Carbolic Smoke Ball Company as a corporate vehicle for his invention, a device which he claimed prevented influenza. Roe was cynically cashing in on the Russian Flu pandemic, which had killed over a million people across Europe in the previous six years. As part of its advertising, the company offered a reward of £100 to any buyer who followed the instructions and subsequently contracted the disease, and claimed that '£1,000 Is deposited with the ALLIANCE BANK, REGENT-STREET, showing our sincerity in the matter.'

Mrs Louisa Carlill, the wife of a solicitor, purchased one and dutifully followed the instructions, but contracted influenza

---

[11] [1893] 1 QB 256.
[12] John Randall QC, 'When Louisa Carlill caught the flu', in *Cases that Changed Our Lives, vol II*.

nevertheless. She recovered, presumably due to non-smokeball-related methods, and claimed the reward. When the company refused to pay, she sued them for breach of contract. She won in the High Court and the company appealed to the Court of Appeal.

The company offered two defences to Carlill's claim. First, it argued that the promised reward was a mere 'puff' (pun excused) not intended to be taken literally, but (to use a probably anachronistic example) was instead along the lines of a house offered as a 'handyman's dream'. Secondly, the company argued that it was not possible to contract with the whole world. Therefore, Carlill could not establish a legal relationship with the company on which to found her claim.

The Court of Appeal had no difficulty in rejecting both defences. As to the first, it pointed out that the advertisement was couched in serious terms. What particularly resonated with the judges was the statement about the money being deposited in the bank. It was also observed that if the company was making money out of its outlandish promise of a reward, then it could not complain when held to its word.

The judgment in this respect is often said to be the foundation of the modern contractual requirement of 'intention to create legal relations', though there were examples of earlier judges employing similar reasoning.

As to the second defence, the company complained that it had never heard of Carlill before the claim, so how could it have been said to have contracted with her?

Carlill successfully countered that the advertisement was a 'unilateral contract' (seemingly an oxymoron) in which an offer had been made to the whole world, and it had been accepted by her in legally binding form when she purchased the device and used it as instructed. Bowen LJ put it in these terms: 'why should not an offer be made to all the world which is to ripen into a contract with anybody who comes forward and performs the condition?'

The company also offered some more technical arguments, pointing out that it could not be sure Carlill had complied with the instructions, and that the timing of the agreement was unclear, since it was not certain how long the offer would last, how soon the customer had to contract influenza after using the device, and so on. The Court of Appeal brushed all those aside, giving a good illustration of a practical approach overriding doctrinal technicalities. Carlill had won a famous victory.

The approach of the Court of Appeal has often been said to represent an important step in the formation of modern contract law, which offers 'both a framework for understanding the social relations thrown up by a market economy and a theory for the legitimate exercise of state power'.[13]

The case was also a step towards the modern system of consumer law, but not the most important; a better candidate would probably be Mrs Donoghue's snail-related action found in Part VII of this book. But I also suspect that the fact of a respectable housewife being taken in by a charlatan would have had some influence on the judges when faced with the more technical aspects of the defence: had the claim been brought instead by a large and sophisticated company who had made a bad purchase, the judges might have told it to live with its own foolishness.

Either way, the case still stands as a classic example of the two separate questions of (i) distinguishing between mere advertising guff and actual binding promises; and (ii) the concept of a unilateral contract.

Like the agile businessman he seems to have been, Roe tried to use his court defeat to his advantage. He formed a new company to sell the smokeball and boasted that of more than a thousand sold under the old terms, only three people had claimed the reward, thus proving its efficacy. But he did not enjoy success for long, since he died of tuberculosis before the end of the century.

Louisa Carlill, on the other hand, lived until 1942, by which time she had reached the grand age of 96. As noted by the

---

[13] Hugh Collins, *The Law of Contract: Law in Context*, 4th edn. LexisNexis UK (2003), pp 5–6, quoted by Randall, op. cit.

legal historian A. W. B 'Brian' Simpson,[14] her death certificate recorded the chief cause as old age, but one other factor as well – 'influenza'.

---

[14]   Brian Simpson, 'Quackery and Contract Law: The Case of the Carbolic Smoke Ball' (1985) 14 *Journal of Legal Studies* 345 at 389, quoted by Randall, op. cit. Simpson also pointed out that Carlill had moved to the Kentish coast, a lively environment during the Battle of Britain.

J'accuse

One of the greatest of all legal sagas is that of Captain Dreyfus, the unfortunate French soldier wrongly convicted of leaking military secrets in the late 19th century. There are many reasons for the story's enduring fame. Chiefly it has become shorthand for the sort of institutional failure where an individual injustice is perpetuated for no reason other than that it does not suit the institution to undo it. In *Standpoint Magazine* in November 2012, for example, the journalist Nick Cohen called the Salman Rushdie affair 'the Dreyfus case of our age', given the supine reaction on the part of British intellectuals to calls for Rushdie's murder.

More recently, assuming even a fraction of the allegations to be true, the Jimmy Savile scandal may constitute another example, albeit in the opposite form: in Rushdie's case, as in Dreyfus's own, an innocent man was virtually hung out to dry because the intelligentsia found it too inconvenient to defend him, whereas with Savile an apparently guilty man was allowed to continue offending because it did not suit the institutions with whom he dealt to confront him.[15]

The story of Dreyfus begins with the Franco-Prussian War of 1870–71, when as a child he witnessed occupying Prussian troops in his home town in Alsace and vowed to join the French army. He did so in due course and fashioned a strong academic and service record. In the 1890s, however, he was court-martialled for espionage, accused of selling artillery secrets to the Germans. He was convicted, publicly humiliated and sentenced to life imprisonment on Devil's Island, the French penal island later of *Papillon* fame.

His supporters soon amassed evidence proving that another officer had been responsible for the leaks. Obviously an appeal

---

[15] Savile, a media personality in Britain well known in the latter half of the 20th century, did a substantial amount of fundraising for various hospitals and other charitable causes, and threatened to withdraw support if anyone questioned him. He also threatened the use of the libel courts. Once he died, and both threats were therefore spent, an extraordinary number of allegations of sexual abuse were made about him, some going back decades.

and restoration of Dreyfus' good name should have followed promptly, but there was a problem: it was considered by the upper echelons of the French army, and enough of French *haute société* as a whole, that the institution of the army could not suffer a blow to its reputation of the scale which would be inflicted were the injustice to be admitted. Instead they decided to perpetrate the same injustice all over again: Dreyfus' original conviction was quashed but at a subsequent court martial he was found guilty again.

By this time the case had become a *cause célèbre*, and French society had started to fracture along pro- and anti-Dreyfus lines. Prominent amongst the former was the author Émile Zola, who wrote the legendary '*J'accuse*' open letter to President Faure, alleging a cover-up amongst senior officers. For his trouble he was tried for criminal libel, though he avoided prison by fleeing to England. Meanwhile, Major Henri, whose evidence had been prominent in securing the original conviction, committed suicide. The Minister for War, General Mercier, on the other hand, remained unrepentant, warning that if Dreyfus was found innocent 'the entire German army would be over the border within weeks.'

Eventually the weight of evidence began to tell. In 1899, Dreyfus returned to France for a retrial. Though found guilty again, he was pardoned and released. In 1906, after yet another appeal, he was finally declared innocent. He was also awarded the *Légion d'honneur* and restored to officer status. He later served with distinction at Verdun during the Great War before dying in 1935.

It is probably just as well he never lived to see what happened just a few years later, when, as we all know, for reasons unconnected with him, the German army once more came over the border, this time sweeping to Paris within weeks. Ironically many former anti-Dreyfusards then became involved in the Vichy regime, and they turned a blind eye to Dreyfus's Jewish granddaughter being sent to Auschwitz.

The French army's name was severely damaged by the Dreyfus affair, though not quite in the way feared by Mercier and his fellow apologists. Instead it lost much of its reputation for integrity, both nationally and internationally, and a fair degree of soul searching followed. It was clear that at least part of the problem had been rank anti-Semitism amongst authority – something, incidentally, of which Dreyfus had been a victim even before the affair, being marked down at the *École Supérieure de Guerre* in 1892 because, according to an examiner, 'Jews were not desired'. Hence the developing concept of *laïcité* gained additional currency – and even before the final acquittal of Dreyfus the 1905 Law on the Separation of the Churches and State had been passed (though also to restrain Catholic influence).

Various other things great and small can trace their origin to the Dreyfus affair, even the *Tour de France* (originally a fundraising activity of a newspaper, *L'Auto*, set up by anti-Dreyfusards to counter the pro-Dreyfus *Le Vélo*). The *Daily Mail* famously reproduced the *J'accuse* headline in relation to Stephen Lawrence's alleged murderers. But the real legacy, as mentioned, derives from the fact that an institution perpetuated an individual injustice to save its own face, only to suffer greater damage when the truth finally emerged.

As for later parallels, we might add to the Rushdie and Savile affairs various sordid sagas such as the Catholic Church sex scandals, which savaged that institution's reputation in many countries (particularly Ireland, where previously it had held the nearest position to a *de facto* theocracy in a modern English-speaking state), or the repeated establishment obstinacy over police corruption in the United Kingdom which led to the creation of the Criminal Cases Review Commission. It seems that as long as we have institutions of any sort we will have Drefuysian scandals.[16]

[16]   Published in the *New Law Journal*, vol 162, 16 November 2012, p 1434.

Part II: Crime and Punishment

INTRODUCTION

In 1934, in her preface to an anthology of short detective stories, Dorothy L. Sayers wrote 'Death in particular seems to provide the minds of the Anglo-Saxon race with a greater fund of innocent amusement than any other single subject.' It is safe to say that not much has changed: literature on murder mysteries, both fictional and true, continues to appear in at least as much profusion as in Sayers' day. Some very well-known murders are considered in this part: the deaths of Julia Wallace and Honoria Parker have both given rise to a number of plays, documentaries, books and films.

The Wallace case is a classic 'whodunit'. The Parker/Hulme murder, on the other hand, never involved any doubt about the perpetrators; instead, the interest in the case derives from the unusual and – particularly for the time – shocking background facts.

The case of *R v Collins*, on the other hand, had background facts that amounted to farce, and it has entered law student legend accordingly. But there was also a serious crime involved. So too the case of *R v Bentham* – and in that instance, I have to say that I do not think the judgment of the House of Lords adequately addressed the issue.

Finally in this part is the case of Alan Turing, a great British hero who, like Oscar Wilde, was a victim of the unjust offence involving consenting adult males, under the Criminal Offences Act 1885. In the early 21st century, several decades after his death, a campaign began for Turing to be given a posthumous pardon. I had the following letter published in *The Times*:[1]

> Many arguments have been raised by your recent correspondents concerning Alan Turing, but the nub of the case can be stated simply. Turing was not wrongly convicted because he was a genius; he was wrongly convicted because his actions should

---

[1] Published on 26 July 2013.

never have been a crime in the first place. His conviction would have been equally unjust had he been a drunken layabout instead of a national hero.

There is no need for a retrospective pardon, because Parliament has already made clear that Turing and others should not have been convicted, by repealing the relevant offence, and by the passage of various equality laws in recent years.

The article makes the same argument in an expanded form. I should note that one positive side effect of the campaign was that many more people became aware of Turing's life and achievements. But it did not detract from the point that Turing's case should have been treated no differently from anyone else's.

The Telephone Murder

There may be some English murders that are more famous than that of Julia Wallace in 1931. But there can be very few famous murders that are more *English*, for the crime took place in a setting of such stereotypical suburban blandness that it might have been created for a sketch by Ronnie Barker or Monty Python.

The enduring fame of the Wallace murder derives from the fact that so many of the facts are uncontested and yet opinions differ so wildly on who committed it. No less an authority than the author Raymond Chandler described it as the greatest murder-mystery in history.

William Wallace led a life that he himself described as 'ill-starred'. He had been invalided out of the Great War. He had a jobbing career in different fields, and at the time of Julia's murder he was working as an insurance agent. His hobbies included chess and the violin, both of which he played with more enthusiasm than ability. By his own admission marrying Julia counted as his life's greatest achievement.

Whether Julia shared that view is debatable, given that by the rigid standards of the class system of her day she had married beneath herself, William's means being distinctly less than those of her father. The couple had no children.

One day, upon arriving at his chess club, William was given a message that had been left by telephone. It asked him to come to an address on the other side of town after work the next day for a potential insurance deal. He recognised neither the name of the caller nor the address. Nevertheless, the next day he attempted to keep the requested appointment, before discovering that the address was fictitious. Upon returning home he found Julia lying on the floor: she had been battered to death by a blunt instrument.

There was no sign of forced entry and only a paltry sum of money missing. There was no murder weapon and no suspect other than William himself.

All hinged on the identity of the telephone caller. Quite coincidentally, the line had been undergoing maintenance at the time, which enabled the police to trace the call to a kiosk very close to the Wallace home. Either William had made the call himself to provide an alibi, or it had been someone else getting him out of the way. Whichever was the case, in all probability the caller was the killer, or at least an accomplice.

The police calculated that it was possible for Wallace to have left the message and arrived at the club when he did, though only marginally. The staff member at the club who took the message said the caller was not Wallace, though one wonders how conclusive that view could have been with 1930s' technology and the resultant inferior sound quality.

The same applied to the day of the murder: it would have been possible for William to have committed the crime before leaving the house on the false trail of the insurance appointment, but only just, especially given that William was hardly a robust physical specimen capable of a short burst of violent energy followed by a speedy disposal of the murder weapon and any other incriminating evidence.

In the event, William was charged, tried and convicted, despite the judge's summing up being mostly in his favour. He was then sentenced to death, but managed to appeal successfully.[2] His appeal made a small footnote in legal history since it was the first time the Criminal Court of Appeal had allowed an appeal because the weight of evidence did not exclude reasonable doubt, rather than because there had been a defect in the trial process or similar.

Since then, the murder has formed the basis of two television series and a number of books, and many contrasting theories have been advanced in each. Two modern attempts are the book *The Telephone Murder* by Ronald Bartle,[3] a retired barrister and former magistrate, and an article in 2013 for the *Sunday Times* by the crime writer P. D. James.[4]

---

[2] The appeal case was reported as *R v Wallace* (1931) 23 Cr App R 32.
[3] Published by Wildy, Simmonds & Hill in 2012.
[4] P. D. James (Baroness James of Holland Park), 'Murder, She Wrote',

Bartle criticised a number of previous theories, including the most popular alternative suspect of Richard Parry (a former business associate of Wallace, who supposedly had an axe to grind for work reasons, or who might – as some have speculated – have been having an affair with Julia. He also did not give a consistent story to police about his movements). That would leave William Wallace himself, but it has to be said Bartle produced neither a smoking gun nor a compelling rebuttal of the weaknesses of the case against Wallace.

On the other hand, as Bartle acknowledged, the chief problem with any alternative to Wallace is the lack of motive. It is not difficult to imagine a motive for Wallace himself: perhaps Julia had been unfaithful, or humiliated him remorselessly about his failure to keep her in a lifestyle to which she had previously been accustomed. But why would anyone else want Julia dead? The Wallaces scarcely had enough possessions to justify a potentially violent robbery, and jilted adulterers (if there was one) are much rarer murderers than cuckolded husbands. The finger then points back to William, though it is hard to disagree with Raymond Chandler's verdict that '[William] Wallace could not have done it – but neither could anyone else'.

On further investigation I discovered that Bartle omitted some interesting findings, including the contention that Julia Wallace was much older than she claimed, though I think he was right not to spend long on the idea that Wallace had an accomplice (who could Wallace have known that would have agreed to such an act? If Wallace duped them into assisting what they thought was a more innocent deception, would they have stayed silent afterwards? That is, unless they were some extremely hardened criminal, but is it likely Wallace knew how to contact such an individual?).

Baroness James's theory was more imaginative. She suggested that the caller was not, as everyone had always assumed, the killer or an accomplice. Instead, she reasoned it was Parry, intending to send Wallace on a wild goose chase, but only as a practical joke, not to get him out of the house to

Sunday Star Times, 27 October 2013, p 46. Baroness James died in 2014.

facilitate Julia's murder. Wallace, desperately miserable in his failed life, then seized the opportunity to do something he had been presumably dreaming of doing for a long time, and killed Julia before leaving for the non-existent appointment. James pointed out that Parry had reason to dislike Wallace, but that it would be a stretch to find anything strong enough to cause him to murder Julia.

I would agree that Wallace had the most obvious motive, based primarily on Julia's reduced circumstances and the consequent inferred lack of marital harmony. But I have to say that the James thesis otherwise seems implausible. The suggested practical joke was absurdly weak, and if Wallace did not know that Parry had been responsible, it is hard to see Parry getting much satisfaction out of it. A few hours wasted, a small hope of a sale dashed, and the cost of the use of public transport would not exactly have added up to the worst day of William Wallace's life, and if he did not know of the connection it would not have prompted him to feel any remorse for his dealings with Parry.

James admitted that she was only offering speculation, and therefore accepted that the right result legally was eventually reached (after Wallace won his appeal), since there was always reasonable doubt.

That was fair enough, though I suspect both James and Bartle would have admitted they had not had the last word – but then again nor will anyone else in a case the trial judge rightly described as 'unexampled in the annals of crime'.[5]

---

[5] An earlier version of this chapter was published in the *Criminal Bar Quarterly*, Issue 2, Summer 2013, p 14 and also in *Criminal Law & Justice Weekly*, 9 December 2014.

Death in the Afternoon

I have previously written[6] about the director Peter Jackson's film *Brain Dead*, which was the subject of legal proceedings thanks to a rather thin-skinned viewer. Jackson's breakthrough film was *Heavenly Cretures*, a film based on one of New Zealand's most famous true crimes, the Parker-Hulme murder of 1954.

Juliette Hulme and Pauline Parker were schoolgirls in Christchurch in the early 1950s. They formed an intensely close personal friendship, and spent much time together inventing their own fantasy world. Much speculation has since occurred as to whether their relationship was sexual; either way there is no doubt they became extremely close, to the increasing consternation of their respective parents. Eventually it was announced that Parker's family would be moving overseas. The girls were horrified at the prospect of separation – to the point where they resorted to murder. They hoped that by killing Parker's mother Honoria and making it look like an accident, they would be able to thwart the move. They recorded their plans in some detail and with some anticipation in their diaries. On the day in question they went for a walk in Victoria Park, a picturesque area in the Port Hills near Christchurch. They distracted Honoria Parker before hitting her repeatedly with a brick in a stocking. She died a slow and agonising death.

The girls were arrested almost immediately and charged with murder. Due to their age, they were not permitted to give evidence at the trial. There was no dispute that they had killed Honoria; the only issue was whether they should be found not guilty by reason of insanity. In the event both were convicted. They could not receive the death penalty, again because of their ages. Instead they were sentenced to be detained at Her Majesty's Pleasure. They were held in separate prisons and not permitted any contact with each other. The state took great care over their education while they were incarcerated, and as

---

[6]   See *Cases, Causes and Controversies*, Chapter 33.

it happened each was only detained for about five years before being released and given a new identity.

Coincidentally, both eventually moved to Britain, though they apparently never made contact again. Both lived anonymously until the early 1990s when, after *Heavenly Creatures* was released, they were tracked down by investigative reporters. Parker was working as a riding instructor in England, and refused to speak publicly. Hulme, on the other hand, attracted particular attention because she was revealed to be the well-known novelist Anne Parry, whose speciality is murder-mysteries. She was persuaded to give interviews and has done so on several occasions in recent years. Among other things, she has denied that her relationship with Parker was sexual and has decried the fact that she was not permitted to speak in her own defence at the trial, though she has never denied committing the crime.

To understand how the Parker-Hulme murder was perceived at the time and since requires some understanding of the time and place in which it occurred. New Zealand in the 1950s was an extraordinary homogenous society – ethnically, ethically, religiously and socially. Maori were the only significant ethnic minority, and official policy towards them (abandoned from about the 1980s) was mostly one of cultural assimilation. Aside from the odd bit of Maori tokenism, New Zealand's media and public institutions were rigidly conformist. To modern eyes, the society was deeply sexist, while homosexuality was considered a form of mental illness, attracting complete social ostracism. Two schoolgirls committing murder would have been bad enough, therefore, but any inference that they had what the Victorians would have called an 'unnatural friendship' would have rendered the affair completely beyond the pale.

That apparently suffocating social rigidity has caused a number of modern writers to view the crime in something of a revisionist light, though I cannot agree with the rather extreme argument advanced by some that the moral climate, however oppressive, justified or even mitigated the murder of an innocent person. Instead, I would suggest that there are two contrasting parts to the equation. On the one hand, it is a relief that the sexism and homophobia of the 1950s have largely vanished.

On the other hand, the crime rate generally in New Zealand in the 1950s was astonishingly low, even allowing for differences in reporting and changes in attitudes to certain crimes (in the 1950s making allegations of sexual abuse or domestic violence, for example, would have been extremely difficult for the victims). Unemployment levels were far lower, as was welfare dependence in general, so in several important respects a utilitarian would have grounds to say that 1950s New Zealand was a happier and more prosperous place than now.

Moreover, while it was clearly wrong for Parker and Hulme not to have been permitted to give evidence in their defence (it would probably have made no difference to the outcome, but that is not the point), the actual outcome of the criminal justice process in their case does not seem open to criticism. Both served a very short sentence by the standards of murder convictions; they were educated to a high level in the process; and they were well integrated back into society given that they have each led prosperous and law-abiding lives ever since – in other words, a model example of punishment and rehabilitation.

In the present day, therefore, they might have had a fairer trial but, paradoxically, not necessarily a fairer result.[7]

---

[7] Published in the *New Law Journal*, vol 163, 22 February 2013, p 214.

Mistaken Identity

'This is about as extraordinary a case as my brethren and I have ever heard either on the Bench or while at the Bar' began Lord Justice Edmund Davies in the case of *R v Collins*.[8] His words remain true more than forty years later: of all cases in this book, the facts of *Collins* are about the most bizarre, and they provide substantial support for the cliché about truth being stranger than fiction.

Stephen Collins was charged with burglary with intent to commit rape, under s 9 of the Theft Act 1968. He was convicted and appealed to the Court of Appeal. Edmund Davies LJ set out the background to the case as follows:

> Let me relate the facts. Were they put into a novel or portrayed on the stage, they would be regarded as being so improbable as to be unworthy of serious consideration and verging at times on farce. At about 2 o'clock in the early morning of Saturday 24th July of last year, a young lady of 18 went to bed at her mother's home in Colchester. She had spent the evening with her boyfriend. She had taken a certain amount of drink, and it may be that this fact affords some explanation of her inability to answer satisfactorily certain crucial questions put to her.
>
> She has the habit of sleeping without wearing night apparel in a bed which is very near the lattice-type window of her room. At one stage on her evidence she seemed to be saying that the bed was close up against the window which, in accordance with her practice, was wide open. In the photographs which we have before us, however, there appears to be a gap of some sort between the two, but the bed was clearly quite near the window.
>
> At about 3.30 or 4 o'clock she awoke and she then saw in the moonlight a vague form crouched in the open window. She was unable to remember, and this is important, whether the form was on the outside of the window sill or on that part of the sill which was inside the room, and for reasons which will later become clear, that seemingly narrow point is of crucial importance.

[8] [1973] QB 100.

The young lady then realised several things: first of all that the form in the window was that of a male; secondly that he was a naked male; and thirdly that he was a naked male with an erect penis. She also saw in the moonlight that his hair was blond. She thereupon leapt to the conclusion that her boyfriend with whom for some time she had been on terms of regular and frequent sexual intimacy, was paying her an ardent nocturnal visit. She promptly sat up in bed, and the man descended from the sill and joined her in bed and they had full sexual intercourse. But there was something about him which made her think that things were not as they usually were between her and her boyfriend. The length of his hair, his voice as they had exchanged what was described as 'love talk', and other features led her to the conclusion that somehow there was something different. So she turned on the bed-side light, saw that her companion was not her boyfriend. So she slapped the face of the intruder, who was none other than the Appellant. He said to her, 'Give me a good time tonight', and got hold of her arm, but she bit him and told him to go. She then went into the bathroom and he promptly vanished.

The complainant said that she would not have agreed to intercourse if she had known that the person entering her room was not her boyfriend. But there was no suggestion of any force having been used upon her, and the intercourse which took place was undoubtedly effected with no resistance on her part.

Farcical as they were, the events were also very unfortunate for all concerned. Collins was remorseful, particularly when he found himself charged with a serious criminal offence. His version of events was that he knew the complainant, having worked around the house. He was drunk on the night in question. He saw a light on in the complainant's bedroom, and climbed up a ladder more in hope than expectation. On seeing her naked he returned to the bottom of the ladder and stripped off all his clothes bar his socks, his reasoning being that if the girl's mother entered the bedroom it would make for an easier getaway for some reason than if he was in bare feet. On that point Edmund Davies LJ recorded: 'That is a matter about which we are not called upon to express any view, and would in any event find ourselves unable to express one.'

Collins then claimed that the complainant had awoken as he was pulling himself into the room from the window sill. She had seemed to pull him into the bed, which rather stunned him as he had assumed she 'wouldn't want to know me' (raising the question as to why he had stripped down to his socks). The crux of his defence was that he had never intended to force himself on anyone and would not have had sex with the complainant had she not seemed willing.

Having set out the facts, Edmund Davies LJ turned to whether there had been an offence committed. That was a matter of technical, black letter law. Section 9 of the 1968 Act provided that a person was guilty of burglary if he entered any building or part of a building as a trespasser and with the intention of committing rape.

Thus, three elements had to be proved by the prosecution: (i) that the offender had entered a building; (ii) that he was trespassing by doing so; and (iii) that he had the intention of committing rape.

There was no doubt that Collins had entered the bedroom and thus the first element of the offence was satisfied.

As to the second element, the key question was where exactly Collins was at the moment when, according to him, the complainant indicated that she was welcoming him. Was he kneeling on the sill outside the window? Or was he already inside the room, having climbed through the window frame, and kneeling upon the inner sill?

The point at which one actually 'enters' a building had never arisen in a case before, though textbooks offered differing opinions. Edmund Davies LJ held that there could not be a conviction for entering premises 'as a trespasser' within the meaning of s 9 of the Act unless the person entering, 'does so knowing that he is a trespasser and nevertheless deliberately enters, or, at the very least, is reckless as to whether or not he is entering the premises of another without the other party's consent'.

So the question was whether, at the point of entering the room, Collins had known that he was not welcome, or had recklessly disregarded the fact. Had the bed been on the opposite side of the room to the window, and Collins therefore not received the mistaken welcome until he was inside the premises, then the offence might have been established. But, according to his account, the complainant had clearly welcomed him in before he had crossed the threshold (as it were) of the windowsill. That being so, Edmund Davies LJ ruled:

> If the jury thought he might be truthful in that assertion, they would need to consider whether or not, although entirely surprised by such a reception being accorded to him, this young man might not have been entitled reasonably to regard her action as amounting to an invitation to him to enter.

Therefore:

> Unless the jury were entirely satisfied that the Appellant made an effective and substantial entry into the bedroom without the complainant doing or saying anything to cause him to believe that she was consenting to his entering it, he ought not to be convicted of the offence charged. The point is a narrow one, as narrow maybe as the window sill which is crucial to this case. But this is a criminal charge of gravity and, even though one may suspect that his intention was to commit the offence charged, unless the facts show with clarity that he in fact committed it he ought not to remain convicted.

And so the appeal succeeded.

As bizarre and amusing as it all was, it is important not to lose sight of the fact that what occurred must have been traumatizing for the complainant. Even if in the eyes of the law no crime had been committed, it is unlikely that she would have seen it that way.

The problem is that a criminal conviction cannot be imposed on a defendant solely because the complainant has been morally wronged. Collins was presumably not charged with rape because of the complainant's apparent consent. (Though it should be noted that since the complainant had been asleep just before he arrived, there is a question as to whether she was in a position to give informed consent.) Hence he was charged under s 9 of the 1968 Act – the criminal conduct being trespassing with the *intention* of committing rape. Since it could not be established beyond reasonable doubt that he had been trespassing, he had to be acquitted.

And therein lies the price of the rule of law: sometimes, an apparently unjust result is inevitable.

Hands Up!

Some parents take the view that their children are not to be given any toy soldiers or guns and are not to be encouraged to play any games involving war or violence of any sort. I know of two who implemented such a policy, only to find to their dismay that their children easily circumvented the ban with their own imagination, using any form of improvised device as a pretend gun, be it a broken broom handle, a toilet roll or whatever.

Such activities might or might not be harmless fun for children, but for any adult, believing that someone is holding an actual firearm is presumably just as terrifying as actually facing someone with one. That is why possession of imitation firearms has long been a serious criminal offence. And it is also why the case of *R v Bentham*[9] involves a puzzling decision that, in my respectful opinion, was not quite as obvious as a panel of distinguished judges seemed to think.

Bentham had broken into the home of the victim (a Mr Angus) and woken him up. As later described in court:

> Bentham had his hand inside his jacket, forcing the material out so as to create the impression that he had a gun. In a loud and aggressive manner he said: 'I want every penny in the house and all the jewellery off her neck, or else I'll shoot you.'
> In fear, Mr Angus handed over a significant amount of money.

Bentham was charged in the Crown Court with possession of an imitation firearm, contrary to s 17(2) of the Firearms Act 1968 (the Act). That section provided: 'If a person at the time of committing [robbery] has in his possession a firearm or imitation firearm, he shall be guilty of an offence . . .'

'Imitation firearm' was defined in s 5(4) of the Act as 'any thing which has the appearance of a firearm'.

At first glance, it would seem that the case was a straightforward one: Bentham tricked Angus into believing he had a firearm, and Angus had handed over a lot of money on the basis of that belief. Yet Bentham appealed his conviction,

---

[9]   [2005] 2 All ER 65.

claiming that because he had not used an object to give the appearance of a firearm, but rather his own finger, he could not have satisfied the requirements of the Act. That was because he could not be said to be in 'possession' of his own finger, which was therefore not a 'thing' for the purposes of s 5(4).

The Court of Appeal swiftly knocked that argument down. In a concise and tightly-reasoned judgment, Lord Justice Kennedy said:

> If the matter had gone to trial ... the jury would have had to consider whether when at the critical time when threatening Mr Angus and his partner the appellant had in his possession an imitation firearm. That is to say, having regard to the statutory definition, anything which had the appearance of a firearm. We cannot see that it mattered whether or not that item was made of plastic, or wood, or simply anorak fabric stiffened by a finger, if in the opinion of the jury at the relevant time it had the appearance of a firearm then, in our judgment, they were entitled to find that the offence was made out. Accordingly, we dismiss this appeal against conviction.

Bentham appealed to the House of Lords, where somewhat surprisingly he received a unanimous decision in his favour. Lord Bingham gave the only reasoned judgment,[10] which like Kennedy LJ's was very short and to the point. He stated:

> One cannot possess something which is not separate and distinct from oneself. An unsevered hand or finger is part of oneself. Therefore one cannot possess it. Resort to metaphor is impermissible because metaphor is a literary device which draftsmen of criminal statutes do not employ. What is possessed must under the definition be a thing. A person's hand or fingers are not a thing. If they were regarded as property for purposes of s 143 of the 2000 Act the court could, theoretically, make

---

[10] Lord Rodger added a judgment which amounted to not much more than a coda: 'My Lords, dominus membrorum suum suorum nemo videtur: no one is to be regarded as the owner of his own limbs says Ulpian (D9.2.13. pr). Equally, we may be sure, no one is to be regarded as being in possession of his own limbs. The Crown's argument, however, depends on the contrary, untenable, proposition that, when carrying out the robbery, the appellant had his own fingers in his possession in terms of the Firearms Act 1968. I agree with my noble and learned friend, Lord Bingham of Cornhill, that for this reason the appeal should be allowed.'

an order depriving the offender of his rights to them and they could be taken into the possession of the police.

We therefore have the unusual situation where on very simple facts four judges (in the Crown Court and the Court of Appeal) thought one thing, but five judges (in the House of Lords) quite another.

I will try and state my own view just as succinctly as all the courts did. The Act required the defendant to have been in 'possession' of a 'thing' which gave the appearance of a firearm. No one disputed that Bentham had given that appearance. It might be said that his finger was not something of which he was in 'possession', although there remains the point that people are occasionally said to lose a limb, which implies that they had previously been in 'possession' of it. But I do not think that matters either way. The point is that Bentham was using two things to create the illusion of the gun – his hand and his anorak. There can be no dispute that he was 'in possession' of the latter, which, when stiffened by his finger, was just as much a material object as an imitation firearm or anything else.

Therefore, with respect, the Court of Appeal's judgment is to be preferred and Bentham should have been convicted.[11]

[11]   I should note for completion that just because Bentham escaped the firearms charge does not mean he would have walked free; he would still have been convicted of burglary and possibly other offences as well.

Righting Past Wrongs

Alan Turing was one of the greatest British heroes in the Second World War. His work at Bletchley Park was instrumental in cracking the Enigma code. After the war his contribution to computer science was at least as significant, reflected in the fact that he is known today as the father of computer programming.

But there was a tragic ending to his life story. He was convicted in 1952 of homosexual offences ('gross indecency' between men, contrary to s 11 of the Criminal Law Amendment Act 1885, the same offence of which Oscar Wilde had been convicted more than half a century earlier) and was given chemical castration as an alternative to prison. He died shortly thereafter and the received view (though not unanimous) is that it was suicide.

In recent years a campaign has begun for Turing to be given a posthumous pardon. In September 2009, the Prime Minister, Gordon Brown, issued an apology for Turing's treatment, though not a formal pardon. In 2012, the centenary of Turing's birth, a suggested pardon was rejected by Lord McNally, Minister of State for Justice, on the ground that Turing had been properly convicted of the law as it then stood. A private member's bill proposing to grant Turing a statutory pardon was later presented to the House of Lords. An open letter was also published in the *Daily Telegraph*, signed by a number of leading scientists including Professor Stephen Hawking, repeating the call for a pardon.

Recently two lawyers, Alex Bailin QC and John Halford, threatened that legal action might follow if the pardon was not forthcoming.[12] They wrote:

> Under section 92 of the Protection of Freedoms Act 2012 a person may apply for their conviction under anti-homosexual

---

[12] Alex Bailin QC and John Halford, 'Brushing off moral case for pardon of Alan Turing may well turn into a legal case', *Oxford Human Rights Hub Blog*, 4 January 2013. See http://ohrh.law.ox.ac.uk/brushing-off-moral-case-for-pardon-of-alan-turing-may-well-turn-into-a-legal-case/ (Retrieved 6 February 2015).

laws (including the 1885 Act) to be 'disregarded' if the relevant conduct is no longer an offence. The effect is very similar to a pardon. But section 92 applies only to living persons.

The Government's intention when passing section 92 was to recognise the injustice of repressive old laws – even though they were validly passed at the time. So Lord McNally's moral justification for refusing to pardon Turing no longer holds water. And it is legally unsound too – the power to grant pardons is not restricted by section 92.

It is perverse for the Minister to refuse to pardon Turing for reasons which are diametrically opposed to the law which currently applies to living persons. The point is even stronger because the Minister must exercise his discretion compatibly with the European Convention on Human Rights which does not permit criminal convictions for consensual homosexual acts between adults.

Despite having unqualified admiration for Turing's genius and his life's work, and despite sharing the revulsion at his treatment by the state for what should never have been a crime, I have to say that the campaign for a pardon is misjudged. The fact that Turing was a national hero and the fact that his treatment was disgraceful are two separate points. His trial and punishment were disgraceful not because he was a national hero, but because what he was convicted of should never have been an offence in the first place. An ignorant individual who had never contributed anything to the public good would have been just as wrongly tried and punished as Turing.

Parliament has already implicitly condemned Turing's treatment by decriminalising homosexual conduct and by all of the equality legislation passed since. Those steps have exonerated not just Turing or other famous individuals such as Oscar Wilde, but everyone who was subjected to an unjust law, whether rich or poor, famous or anonymous.

Whether Turing has been adequately recognised for his national contributions is another matter altogether.

The comparison drawn by Bailin and Halford with the well-known case of Derek Bentley is inapposite.[13] The dispute in Bentley's case was whether he had committed the offence, not whether the offence should have existed in law (which in Bentley's case, needless to say, it should have, and still does).

The same reasoning applies to the Great War executions, another comparison made by the same authors. The pardon given in 2006 to those shot at dawn was highly controversial for a number of reasons, none of which arise in Turing's case. I have written about the pardon at greater length elsewhere.[14] Again, however, the dispute in that case concerned whether soldiers were properly convicted, not whether the law against desertion should have existed (and again, it should have and still does, though the death penalty has rightly been abolished).

It would be unjust for Parliament to declare only Turing to have been innocent, and not all the less gifted people who were convicted of the same offence. We should also mention all the others who had to live under an unjust law for decades, though they may have escaped prosecution. Then we could add capital punishment, heresy and every other criminal offence or form of punishment which has since been abolished on moral or other grounds.

Instead, it should be acknowledged that the law as then stood was wrong as applied to everyone – but, as mentioned, that has already been done by abolishing the offence and by the enactment of various equality measures.[15]

Afterword

Turing eventually received a Royal Pardon in December 2013. My view remains unchanged.

---

[13] Bentley was hanged in the 1950s for the murder of a policeman, but his conviction was quashed following a posthumous appeal in 2000. The Court of Appeal only held that he had not had a fair trial, which is not the same as an acquittal. If Bentley had still been alive, he would most probably been retried.
[14] See *Cases, Causes and Controversies*, Chapter 9.
[15] Published in *Criminal Law & Justice Weekly*, vol 177, 16 February 2013, p 105.

Part III: Free Speech

INTRODUCTION

According to the European Court of Human Rights:[1]

> Freedom of expression constitutes one of the essential foundations of a democratic society and one of the basic conditions for its progress and for each individual's self-fulfilment. Subject to paragraph 2 of Article 10, it is applicable not only to 'information' or 'ideas' that are favourably received or regarded as inoffensive or as a matter of indifference, but also to those that offend, shock or disturb. Such are the demands of pluralism, tolerance and broadmindedness without which there is no 'democratic society'. As set forth in Article 10, this freedom is subject to exceptions, which ... must, however, be construed strictly, and the need for any restrictions must be established convincingly ...

That passage is a good summary of the basic idea behind freedom of speech as it as has developed in the West since at least the time of John Milton's *Areopagitica* in 1644. But it is a truism that the question is an easy one in the abstract, and not easy in reality. The essays in this part provide some real-world illustrations.

One of the key questions with freedom of speech is: how far should intolerance be tolerated? The essays in this part provide some real-world examples. Much the same issues arise with religion and the law, as we will see later in the book.

Another interesting question, posed by the first case in this part, *G v St Gregory's Catholic Science College*, is whether different standards apply to children. G claimed that his haircut was a cultural statement. An adult could be expected to be allowed any haircut he or she wished. But schoolchildren are supposed to have a certain appearance, in the form of their uniform (which

---

[1] *Stoll v Switzerland* ([GC] no. 69698/01, § 101, ECHR 2007-V) and in *Mouvement raëlien suisse v Switzerland* ([GC], no. 16354/06, § 48, 13 July 2012).

usually includes restrictions on jewellery), and therefore should not schools be entitled to restrict hairstyles as well?

In addition to the difficulties with the limits of free speech in the abstract, there is the significant practical problem of trying to censor the internet. Various undemocratic nations have tried to censor search engines, and they are not to be admired for doing so. But the result of free (that is, non-censored) access to the internet is free access to material published overseas that might ordinarily be banned, due to libellous or seditious content, breach of copyright, legitimate military secrets, or whatever. Even the most ardent free speech advocates have allowed exceptions on at least some of those grounds.

The response of the authorities to date has been to try and prosecute people found with objectionable material, but the practical difficulties of doing so in an age of social media need no elaboration. There are not enough resources for the police to sift through more than a billion social media posts every day. I suspect the answer will be that certain forms of social media will be presumed to be beyond the reach of the law and thus deemed irrelevant: that is, no one will believe anything on social media unless corroborated by a different source.

Another classic debate involving free speech concerns how far people can bring private actions – for libel, or invasion of privacy, for example – and thereby silence their critics? Later in the book, in the section on civil law, a few classic libel cases are discussed, some of which were understandable, and others ridiculous. I have argued before that English libel law in the 21st century has become too claimant-friendly, and that courts should be more accommodating of controversial or challenging speech. I would add that two procedural reforms would be useful. First, injunctions restraining publication should be prohibited, or at the very least restricted to the most extreme circumstances. Secondly, costs awards should hit unsuccessful claimants in the pocket, to act as a deterrent.

Getting Out of Pupils' Hair

> We can't do it, man! That's discipline! That's like tellin' Gene
> Krupa not to go 'boom boom bam bam bam, boom boom bam
> bam bam, boom boom boom bam ba ba ba ba, da boo boo tss!'
>
> Ned Flanders' father, *The Simpsons*

When the magazine *Punch* was still extant, and still funny (not the same thing in its case), it used to have a column for amusing newspaper headlines or bylines, of the sort that are nowadays found in round-robin emails or social media posts. One I recall was an apparently genuine advertisement offering 'a free set of bass guitar strings with every trumpet purchased'.

Another reported 'schoolboy suspended by his head because of his long hair'. Nowadays the unfortunate pupil would have a legal remedy against the school, whichever way one interprets the headline (double pun acknowledged). If his hair became trapped somewhere, doubtless someone would fashion a personal injury action against the school for negligently failing to remove the hazard. If on the other hand he was excluded from the school for a time because of the length of his hair, then he might have an action following the decision of Mr Justice Collins in *G v St Gregory's Catholic Science College*.[2]

G was a pupil who wanted to wear his hair in a style known as 'cornrows'. Although not explicitly contrary to the school's written policy, it had been made clear at the start of the year (at a meeting at which G and his parents were not present) that cornrows would not be acceptable.

G went to court to challenge the ban by way of judicial review. He contended that the policy constituted indirect discrimination on the ground of his race, contrary to s 19 of the Race Relations Act 1976 and s 85 of the Equality Act 2010. He argued that cornrows were an essential part of his culture and thus any general policy which banned them placed him at

---

[2] [2011] All ER (D) 113 (Jun).

41

a special disadvantage whether that was the intention of the policy or not.

The case might be viewed in different ways, perhaps most simply as one concerning the freedom of a school to set a uniform policy. One might have thought the limits on that freedom should be very broad, but then again not so broad as to include discriminatory aspects. General rules may well inadvertently have that effect: a ruling requiring no hats might clash with some religions, for a start.

Even if the UK were to adopt the French concept of *laïcité* and ban all religious symbols in schools, the issue would still arise in cases such as G's, where the ground of objection was one of 'race' or 'culture' rather than 'religion'.[3]

It certainly was not the intention of the policy in G's case to discriminate against anyone; hence the action G brought complained of indirect rather than direct discrimination. As mentioned, that required G to show that the school had a policy which applied equally to all but which placed one group at a particular disadvantage, and, further, that the policy could not be shown to be a proportionate means of achieving a legitimate aim.

Before going on to rule in G's favour, Collins J held that:

> It is only if there is a genuine cultural and family practice of not cutting males' hair and wearing cornrows that an exception could be made. It would be made clear that the grounds for such an exception would have to be established and that conformity must occur unless to conform was regarded as impossible. There is no reason why hairstyles which might be indicative of gang culture should be permitted.

As a starting point, no one would suggest that a school should discriminate, knowingly or otherwise, against a particular culture. But there remains room for disquiet. It is

---

[3] When I showed a draft of this article to a Nigerian colleague she ridiculed the idea that cornrows – at least in the case of male children – had anything to do with Nigerian culture. I am not qualified to comment on that assertion, but even if she was correct G's argument is still worth considering on the basis that the issue is capable of arising in respect of hairstyles or other forms of appearance that definitely are a part of someone's culture.

almost inevitable that some symbols of importance to some pupils will be excluded by any uniform policy. Collins J said that only 'genuine' cultural symbols or practices could form a ground of challenge. But how is the school to judge what is genuine? What of kilts and tartans, both of which can be said to be an important symbol of Scottish culture now, but neither of which have anything like the ancestry television and films would have us believe?

It seems to me that requiring schools to adjudicate on the genuineness of a particular cultural symbol is akin to the decision in *Nicholson v Grainger plc* (discussed in Chapter 26 of this book) to elevate non-religious belief systems to the status of religions for employment purposes. For an employer to try and determine the status of a belief system is an unwieldy and unnecessary exercise; it will be the same for schools. Immediately after G's case, the well-known human rights barrister Adam Wagner wrote that 'schools will be frantically re-examining their hair and clothing policies for potential discrimination and students dreaming of their day winning against their teachers in court' – not, in my view, the best use of the ever-stretched school resources, to put it mildly.[4]

Many pupils (and adults for that matter) change their cultural, religious and other forms of identity as they go along. Is each new identity to be assessed according to its age, how deeply held it is by the particular pupil and some other criterion or criteria?

Moreover, some practices – cultural or whatever – are contrary to principles of liberty, equality and other values, and will end up being banned, causing accusations of inconsistency concerning what is permitted. The school in G's case clearly had that in mind, since it associated cornrows with the gang culture it was trying hard to eradicate. Collins J dismissed the idea of a would-be skinhead using the decision as a precedent, but not all traditions of shaving heads belong to far-right lunatics, so we might expect problems of consistency at least.

---

[4]   http://ukhumanrightsblog.com/2011/06/20/hey-teacher-leave-those-cornrows-alone/.

The simplest solution would be for schools all to loosen their policies to the point where almost nothing is prohibited – but immediately some pupils will start wearing and displaying things others find offensive (Swastikas, pornography, or anything else a school might find contravening the bounds of decency), leading to more governors' meetings and litigation anyway.

Instead, schools should be given freedom to determine policies and adjudicate exceptions themselves, and anyone who disagrees with a particular policy can either (i) choose a new school, or (ii) consider that it is not always a matter for regret that pupils have restrictions on their personal freedom that adults do not.

Afterword

The case bears superficial similarity to the better-known litigation brought in the name of the schoolgirl Sabina Begum.[5] She wanted to wear a full veil to a state school, in accordance with what she claimed were her religious beliefs. In her case, the school's argument that its uniform policy was reasonable was ultimately accepted by the House of Lords (the school had lost in the Court of Appeal). But it did not win on the basis that it was entitled to set the uniform it felt like and that the religious beliefs of children – in reality, the religious beliefs of the parents – should have no bearing on the situation. Instead, the school won because it satisfied the court that it had already gone to sufficient length to set a reasonable policy: it had consulted with the local religious leaders and agreed on a particular uniform for Muslim girls. It seems to me that the school was asking for trouble in that regard, and that the policy of other countries (notably France and Turkey) of not allowing any religious symbols or dress would be a much fairer solution. It would also be one in keeping with treating all pupils as equal

---

[5] *R (on the application of Begum (Sabina)) v Headmaster and Governors of Denbigh High School)* [2006] UKHL 15. See L. Townley, 'Banning the Jilbad in School – A violation of a pupil's right to manifest religion?' in *Cases that Changed Our Lives vol II*, p 145.

before the law and entitled to choose their own religion when adults, just as they are presumed incompetent to vote until they reach the age 18 and thereafter they are protected by the secret ballot so they can vote for whomever they choose, away from family pressure. These themes will be revisited in the religion and law section later in the book.

Bad Law and the Crown Prosecution Service

I wonder how future generations will look back on the early days of social media. Legal historians will doubtless have much to say about how the law tried to regulate it. One case from the early days of Twitter will doubtless cause some bafflement or amusement. I refer to the infamous trial of Paul Chambers, prosecuted for a tweet which was obviously a joke to all – or, rather, all except a few jobsworths comprising various links in the legal chain. In Chambers' case it seems to me that the ultimate fault lay not so much with the outdated legislation[6] under which he was prosecuted, but rather the manifestly bad decisions of those charged with its enforcement, primarily the Crown Prosecution Service (CPS).

Before his tweeting saga began, Chambers was an anonymous good citizen. He was irked to find one weekend in early 2010 that he could not meet his girlfriend in Belfast as planned because his local airport was closed. He tweeted in frustration: 'Crap! Robin Hood airport is closed. You've got a week and a bit to get your shit together otherwise I'm blowing the airport sky high!!'

At the time he had 600 Twitter followers. None of them thought the tweet to be anything other than an obvious joke – which we may infer from the complete dearth of complaints to the police. It was only five days later, when an off-duty security officer searched for references to the airport and came across the tweet, that it was brought to the authorities' intention. The officer's manager thought it a non-threat, as did the airport police, but nevertheless it was referred to the regional police. Chambers was then arrested under the Criminal Law Act 1977 for a suspected bomb hoax. Despite what appear to have been misgivings of at least one of the investigating officers, the file was referred to the CPS and a prosecution was commenced for the lesser offence of sending by a public electronic communication

---

[6]   The Communications Act 2003, properly called ancient since it predated Facebook and Twitter, which revolutionised the Act's subject matter and rendered it totally out of date. We will return to this point in the next article.

network a message of a 'menacing character' contrary to s 127(1)(a) and (3) of the Communications Act 2003.

In the magistrates' court, Chambers was convicted and fined. His conviction was upheld in the Crown Court, which held that the tweet was 'menacing in its content and obviously so … Any ordinary person reading this would see it in that way and be alarmed'.

Patently that was not true – as we have seen, 600 ordinary people in the form of Chambers' Twitter followers had seen the tweet and not contacted any of the emergency services.

Chambers appealed to the Divisional Court. By this time his he had gained the support of a number of public figures. The comedian Al Murray, for example, observed that it was just as well Twitter had not been around in John Betjeman's day, or the residents of Slough might have exacted revenge for his well-known poem.[7]

The two judges in the Divisional Court were not able to agree, so yet more time, money and stress went into a rehearing in front of a three-judge court, headed by the Lord Chief Justice. Finally, on 27 July 2012, more than two-and-a-half years since the tweet had been made, the appeal was allowed[8] and Chambers reassumed his blameless status in society. The reasoning was pithy: the tweet was an obvious joke and no one could reasonably have thought otherwise. Thus, 'on an objective assessment, the decision of the Crown Court that this 'tweet' constituted or included a message of a menacing character was not open to it (para [34])'.

In 2010 in *Criminal Law & Justice Weekly*,[9] referring to the original conviction, I suggested:

> It is telling that there were much more serious crimes with which Chambers could have been charged (but wasn't) … Combatting terrorism … requires acute judgment on the authorities' part, and the ability to recognise real threats.

---

[7] Murray was referring to Betjeman's well-known comic poem *Slough* (1937), which begins: 'Come friendly bombs and fall on Slough!, It isn't fit for humans now, There isn't grass to graze a cow. Swarm over, Death!

[8] See [2012] All ER (D) 346 (Jul).

[9] Vol 174, p 791.

Equally it requires the ability to recognise blatant non-threats. Retaining a sense of humour wouldn't hurt in that regard.

Lucy Corrin, in a blog on *Halsbury's Law Exchange*, made the point succinctly: 'As Henry Ward Beecher once said: 'A person without a sense of humour is like a wagon without springs – jolted by every pebble in the road' … if we were to prosecute for facetiousness the CPS might find itself overwhelmed'.

She also noted the CPS's own guidance on the issue directed that bomb hoaxes should be prosecuted under the 1977 Act, as the original arresting officers in the Chambers case had thought.

It is true that the right result was reached in the end. But that is not good enough: Chambers should never have had his collar felt in the first place. What singles his case out from ordinary failed prosecutions is the almost total lack of professional or public opinion in support of the prosecution at any stage of proceedings. The question therefore arises as to why that small number of police officers, CPS staff and judicial officers held such a different view.

Chambers himself claimed that before the final appeal the CPS lawyers had told him that they would drop the case, but they were promptly overruled by the Director of Public Prosecutions (DPP). The CPS for its part said in a press release that the DPP:

> did instruct the team managing it to consider conceding the appeal … however, at a later stage the DPP was advised that, as a matter of law, conceding the appeal would not be possible. This is because it was not possible because the key finding of fact in the case was a finding of the Crown Court, which only the High Court could overturn. The DPP accepted that advice and reluctantly agreed that the appeal had to proceed.

The satirical publication *Private Eye*[10] disputed the CPS's version of events, but either way it is an unsatisfactory state of affairs. If the DPP considers that a prosecution brought by his subordinates has been based on incorrect legal advice, then his obligation like any other barrister would be to inform the court.

---

[10] *Private Eye*, No 1320, p 15.

Equally, if it emerges after a conviction that the defendant in fact had a watertight alibi, the DPP would not be expected to contest an appeal.

Why, therefore, should it be any different if the DPP considers (as virtually everyone did in the Chambers case) that the lower court's interpretation of a statute is patently wrong, and that there is no public interest in opposing an appeal? He should certainly not feel compelled to put everyone to the trouble of a contested appeal with the secret hope that he will lose.

The logical course in Chambers' case would have been for the DPP to have told the court that he considered that the prosecution by his subordinates had been ill-advised; that the Crown Court's findings were contrary to a proper interpretation of the statute (not to say absurd); and that accordingly the conviction had been wrongly obtained. One would expect the bench then to have asked some searching questions to satisfy itself that the DPP and not the Crown Court was correct. The appeal was by way of case stated, and useful guidance emerged from the court's answers to those questions, but none of that should have been on Chambers' time.

Instead, the time and money of all concerned went to waste on an unnecessary appeal. It could have been even worse. Suppose that the Divisional Court had somehow been persuaded by the arguments supporting the Crown Court. Suppose too that Chambers' resources and willpower had been exhausted, so that he did not feel able to make any further challenge. He would then have been lumped with a conviction which even the DPP did not support. Comment on the injustice of that result seems superfluous.[11]

---

[11]   Published in *Criminal Law & Justice Weekly*, vol 176, 22 September 2012, pp 556–557.

Free Speech and the Internet

I have always enjoyed reading *Private Eye*, and often particularly enjoy the cover picture and caption. Over the years, some of the covers have strayed very much into bad taste, and I suppose my enjoyment therefore counts as something of a guilty pleasure.

For example, at the time of the Thalidomide scandal, a company executive was shown on the cover exclaiming 'they haven't got a leg to stand on.'

Almost matching that for offence was the picture of a stressed-looking Michael Barrymore[12] after a man, Stuart Lubbock, had been found dead at a party at Barrymore's house. Press reports stated that Lubbock had received a serious sexual assault before his death. The caption had someone asking how he died, with Barrymore responding 'Buggered if I know.'

Then there was a picture of Lord Hutton after his well-known report on Dr David Kelly's death, which largely exculpated the government. The caption read '... and in conclusion, I find Dr Shipman innocent of all charges.'[13]

The *Eye* is no stranger to the courts, though so far as I am aware it has only experienced the libel courts at the Royal Courts of Justice on the Strand rather than the criminal courts along the road at the Old Bailey.

Of course I accept that some people would be grossly offended by the three covers I have mentioned. But I do not accept that the *Eye* should have been prosecuted for any of them. Yet the possibility of any similar items landing the *Eye* in the dock must now be raised, given a recent and very disturbing assault on free speech.

One Matthew Woods, a 20-year-old, was sent to prison for 12 weeks for posting offensive and derogatory comments about the missing five-year-old April Jones on his Facebook page. He

[12] Barrymore was a well-known television presenter in Britain in the 1990s and 2000s.
[13] A reference to Dr Harold Shipman, who was probably Britain's most prolific serial killer, though the total number of his victims will probably never be known.

pleaded guilty to an offence under s 127 of the Communications Act 2003, which prohibited a person sending 'by means of a public electronic communications network a message or other matter that is grossly offensive or of an indecent, obscene or menacing character'.

That was the same Act that was responsible for the infamous Paul Chambers' Twitter trial discussed in the previous chapter. In the case of Chambers, what he wrote was patently not of an indecent, obscene or menacing character, so the Crown Prosecution Service should never have gone near him. In the case of Woods, by contrast, what he wrote was certainly indecent and obscene, so it might be said that there was a *prima facie* case against him. But there were at least five problems.

First, the sentence was wholly disproportionate. There are many worse crimes committed every day, such as those involving actual violence or burglary, which do not result in an automatic custodial sentence.

Second, and more fundamentally, criminalising 'offence' is contrary to the basic idea of freedom of speech, which is that not only 'good' speech is permitted.[14]

Third, there is a simple remedy for those who are offended by rubbish on the internet or elsewhere: switch off or change channels or websites.

Fourth, it is necessary to define what is offensive in the first place, which might not be so obvious, although it was probably not controversial in the case of Woods.

Fifth, and finally, any attempts to ban offensive material on Twitter and Facebook or the internet generally are more or less doomed to fail, because there are many millions of posts every day. The CPS cannot possibly consider every one of them and, besides, any number are generated overseas and thus beyond the jurisdiction of the English courts anyway.

As I said in the introduction to this part of the book, the date of the Communications Act gives a clue about why it was such a problem. It was passed in 2003, and therefore predates both Facebook and Twitter. It is a voice not so much from another age

---

[14] See *Cases, Causes and Controversies*, pp 129–152.

as another epoch in the history of electronic communications. I wonder if those drafting the Act really had any idea of the likely effect of what they were doing.

Afterword

Woods' sentence was reduced on appeal, but his conviction stood – so injustice remained. The Act did then receive some belated attention from Parliament and the CPS.

As Not Seen On Television

What would Lionel Hutz, Homer and Marge's lawyer in the early days of *The Simpsons*, have made of the case of *McEwen v Simmons*?[15] Not much, I suspect: Hutz once said in court of his opposing counsel 'wow, that guy's good, he's going to win', and then conducted a clumsy effort to fabricate evidence, which about sums up most of his legal career.

No doubt therefore one Mr McEwen would have been hoping for better representation when, in February 2008, he was convicted in New South Wales of two offences concerning child pornography. The charges concerned images he possessed in the form of a series of cartoons modelled on members of *The Simpsons*, which showed some of the child characters engaged in sexual acts. McEwen appealed his conviction to the Supreme Court of New South Wales.

The appeal was heard by Adams J, who set out more of the facts as follows:

> The male figures have genitalia which is evidently human, as do the mother and the girl. It was accepted, I think that it is implied – from the television series – that, insofar as cartoon characters might have ages, the young male is about ten years old, the female about eight years old and a female toddler. Leaving such an implication aside, it would be difficult to assign ages to either the young male or the girl, though the latter appears to me to be pre-pubertal and the former less than eighteen ...

The appeal concerned whether a fictional cartoon character was a 'person' within the meaning of the statutory offences or, more precisely, a depiction or representation of such a 'person'.

Adams J observed that the *Simpsons* characters made no pretence of imitating any actual or indeed fictional human beings. (I interpolate that various real people have featured as guests or otherwise been referred to on the programme, although none of the pictures in issue concerned any such depictions.)

---

[15] [2008] NSWSC 1292. I should record that the character of Lionel Hutz was retired after the actor who voiced him, Phil Hartman, was tragically killed.

The *Simpsons* characters have only three fingers and their facial proportions (and often their overall proportions) are markedly different from actual human beings. Adams J attributed some significance to those differences, but concluded:

> [W]hether a person is indeed depicted by any particular semblance or simulacrum of a human being must be a question of fact and degree. Merely to give human characteristics to, say, a rabbit, a duck or a flower, to use some other familiar images, would not suffice if it were fair to say that the subject of the depiction remained a rabbit, a duck or a flower. A stick figure could not, I think, depict a person – though vide the Commonwealth offence – it might well depict a representation of a person. No bright line of inclusion or exclusion can be sensibly described. Of course, because the depiction of a person is an essential element of the offence, it must be proved beyond reasonable doubt. Accordingly, if it were reasonably possible that the depiction is not that of a person, the offence is not proved. It follows that a fictional cartoon character, even one which departs from recognizable human forms in some significant respects, may nevertheless be the depiction of a person within the meaning of the Act.

> [41] In my view, the Magistrate was correct in determining that … the word 'person' included fictional or imaginary characters and the mere fact that the figure depicted departed from a realistic representation in some respects of a human being did not mean that such a figure was not a 'person'.

And so the appeal was dismissed.

Without doubting the case for criminalising child pornography, I have to say I disagree with the decision. There are two reasons to criminalise child pornography. The first is that the creation of actual child pornography – that is, depictions of real children engaged in actual sexual acts – necessarily involves the commission of an imprisonable offence. It seems logical that the images of such acts should also be illegal.

A rather trickier issue comes into play when a picture involves the illusion of child pornography, but where in reality no children were involved. Whether that should make a difference to charges relating to possessing the images is another question, and not one arising in the *McEwen* case.

The second reason to criminalise child pornography is that it might be said that the presence of such imagery in society encourages the commission of crimes against children. If valid, this point would be of equal force whether the pictures are of real events or merely seem to be.

In McEwen's case, however, the pictures were not just wholly fictional creations, they were wholly unrealistic ones as well. Though pictures of the *Simpsons* characters might be intended to represent people, they do not and are not supposed to look very much like real human beings – as was conceded all along in the case.

Indeed, the general unreality of the programme has perhaps allowed the creators to get away with being much more risqué and offensive than they might have been had the programme been a live action or otherwise more realistic one. The characters have not aged in over 25 years; Homer has sustained an impossible number of injuries to go with his generally absurdly improbable adventures; and aliens regularly visit during the Halloween specials. Whatever attributes viewers look for in the programme, reality is presumably not one of them.

To suggest that the images in McEwen's possession constituted child pornography would be akin to arguing that the programme's cartoon-within-a-cartoon of *Itchy & Scratchy* (a ludicrously violent parody of *Tom & Jerry*) amounts to a snuff movie. Or, alternatively, that it encourages parents to allow children to watch violent television, given that Bart and Lisa are dedicated fans of *Itchy & Scratchy*.

McEwen's images might have been lewd, disgusting, outrageous, or at the very least in the worst possible taste. But so are a lot of things in life, and it does not follow that they should all attract criminal sanctions.

Free Speech and the Law Society

The High Court judge Sir Paul Coleridge, who retired in 2013, had some interesting forefathers. They included several judges, including the 19th century Lord Chief Justice Coleridge, who presided over the *Tranby Croft* libel suit found in the first chapter in this book.[16] Even better known in the lineage was the poet Samuel Taylor Coleridge, who managed to weave some interesting legal and moral conundrums into his poem, *The Rime of the Ancient Mariner*.[17]

The 21st century Coleridge J specialised in family law. In the early 2010s, he launched a pressure group called 'The Marriage Foundation' (the Foundation). According to its website,[18] the Foundation was intended 'to be a national champion (advocate) for marriage, strengthening the institution for the benefit of children, adults and society as a whole.'

The website further stated: 'Private and public attitudes need to change; reaffirming marriage as the 'gold standard' for couple relationships is an essential first step.'

Early in 2012, whilst Coleridge J was still on the bench, the Foundation planned to have a conference entitled 'One Man. One Woman. Making the case for marriage'. It booked a venue at the Law Society's headquarters on Chancery Lane. Shortly afterwards, however, the Law Society indicated that it would no longer agree to host the event, on the ground that the event was

---

[16] Coleridge LCJ also heard the classic case of shipwrecked sailors eating the unfortunate cabin boy (*R v Dudley and Stephens*), which gave rise to a great moral and legal issue – whether necessity can be a defence to murder. *See Cases, Causes and Controversies*, Chapter 3.

[17] The poem's conclusion on animal rights – that 'He prayeth best, who loveth best All things both great and small' – was certainly at variance with the received view of the day, which would have been the traditional Judeo-Christian beliefs as expressed in Genesis 1.26.
I also think that the poem's view on crime and punishment – reflected in the execution of two hundred sailors and an endless sentence of purgatory for the Mariner himself – was harsh, even by 18th century standards.

[18] http://www.marriagefoundation.org.uk (Retrieved 12 January 2013).

contrary to the Society's diversity policy 'in espousing an ethos opposed to same-sex marriage'.[19]

A cynic might point out that it was ironic that the Law Society refused to allow a conference *in favour* of the existing law on marriage, when it was happy to host one on assisted suicide, which was *against* the law as it then stood. More to the point, as a supposedly politically neutral body regulating an integral part of the legal profession, perhaps the Law Society should not take positions on political issues at all. Moreover, the views of a sitting High Court judge on an area of policy on which he has experience and expertise would usually be worthy of airing even if one believes them mistaken.

There is a more fundamental point. A diversity policy should not mean the end of freedom of speech or the validity of debate. Rather, it should be the opposite – a diversity of opinion should be valued. The purpose of the Law Society having a diversity policy was to ensure that potential employees of the Law Society, and users of its services, were not discriminated against on any prohibited grounds. That said nothing about requiring everyone to sign up to a particular political or moral agenda, still less that no views contrary to the Society's 'ethos' could be aired.

For example, a university, one would hope, would also have a diversity policy to the same effect. But it would surely not ban debates or seek to limit discussion during lectures and tutorials on the ground that someone might say something contrary to the diversity (or any other) policy.[20]

---

[19]   See eg Geraldine Morris, 'Gay marriage: you say potato and I say potahto', *Halsbury's Law Exchange*, 22 May 2012, http://www.halsburyslawexchange. co.uk/gay-marriage-you-say-potato-and-i-say-potahto/ (Retrieved 23 May 2012).

[20]   Or so I thought when I wrote this article in 2012. There was a dismal saga concerning the segregation of university students in late 2013 and early 2014. The University Council (a body of whom few had heard prior to the row) announced that it was somehow permissible for universities to accede to a request by religious speakers for audiences to be segregated on gender lines. I can do no better than Nick Cohen's articles in the *Spectator* (see 'The segregation of women and the appeasement of bigotry', 3 December 2013 and 'The segregation of women and the appeasement of bigotry at Britain's universities (part two)', 11 December 2013). The University Council tried to hide behind 'legal advice' (either they were untruthful, or the advice was bad,

One assumes that the Law Society does not need any sermons on the value of free speech. No doubt some might respond that the refusal to host the conference did not censor Sir Paul's organisation; any number of other fora were still available to the Foundation without the speech-strings attached. That is true, but it is not the role of the Law Society *qua society* to be taking a prominent position on disputed areas of policy and human rights.[21]

One might also invoke Godwin's law by asking if the Law Society should be compelled to host a conference organised by the National Front or some equivalent. The answer is no, but the Law Society should have a broader, not narrower spectrum of debates it is prepared to host, and The Marriage Foundation is not of a piece with a fascist organisation. It is instead an organisation dedicated to advancing a view shared by millions in the country. Whether one agrees or not, there is clearly a debate to be had which the Law Society should not implicitly be seeking to silence.

It hardly needs pointing out that if debate had been suppressed in a similar fashion in the past by the Law Society and others the issue of gay rights (or assisted suicide for that matter) would never have got off the ground and male homosexual relations might even still be a criminal offence. The Law Society should have allowed the debate, and should have reconsidered what its 'ethos' actually entailed. It should also have recalled that the best way to defeat views it finds objectionable would be to allow them to be aired, and then defeated by the process of rational argument. That, after all, is how same-sex relationships came to be accepted in society in the first place.

and either way the advice should have been disclosed). Eventually, though, the Council realised the moral and intellectual bankruptcy of its position and backed down completely.

[21]   There is a side issue here, namely whether a High Court judge should be involved in this sort of political campaigning. Sir Paul received some censure in this regard from the Judicial Conduct and Investigations Office. See David Barrett, 'Judge Sir Paul Coleridge disciplined for stating views on traditional marriage', *Daily Telegraph*, 17 December 2013.

Afterword

Since the above was written, gay marriage has of course been legalised. Meanwhile, the Society stirred up a different controversy when it issued guidance for Sharia-compliant wills.[22] Under English law, the general principle of testamentary freedom allows testators to be as racist, homophobic, sexist or just about any other '-ist' they choose to be; it is their money after all. Therefore, objectionable aspects of Sharia law (such as discriminating against women) would not technically fall foul of English law in this instance. Legal issues aside, though, the fact that the Law Society was giving support to a belief system that rendered women automatically second-class citizens caused great indignation. After some searing public criticism, the advice was withdrawn, and the Society indicated that nothing would replace it.

---

[22] See for example Carl Gardiner, 'Yesterday's "One Law for All" protest at the Law Society', *Head of Legal*, 29 April 2014, http://www.headoflegal.com/2014/04/29/yesterdays-one-law-for-all-protest-at-the-law-society/#comment-368569 (Retrieved 6 February 2015).

Part IV: Law and War

INTRODUCTION

Went the day well?
We died and never knew
But, well or ill,
Freedom, we died for you

Such are the opening words of one of the greatest of all war films,[1] and they encapsulate what is usually (though not very accurately) said to be the *casus belli* of the Second World War: the fight for individual freedom. The preservation of that freedom during the war itself forms the central theme of the infamous wartime judgment of the House of Lords in *Liversidge v Anderson*, the first case in this part and one of the best known in English history.

As well as its opening lines, the plot of *Went the Day Well?* helps to set the background to Liversidge's case. Based on a short story by Graham Greene, it tells the story of a covert Nazi operation on British soil intended as a precursor to a full-scale German invasion. The aim of the film was to buck up a complacent population so that they would remain alert for possible invasion signs.

With hindsight we know that the threat of invasion had passed by 1942. But no one could have known that with any certainty at the time.[2] It follows that the lesson of the film – that

---

[1] *Went the Day Well?* (1942, dir: Alberto Cavalcanti). The opening lines are taken from an epitaph by John Maxwell Edmonds, which originally appeared in *The Times* on 6 February 1918, and thus during the Great War. Thereafter it appeared in the paper regularly, and was reprised in the Second World War as well. It is sometimes confused with another epitaph also by Edmonds, which read: 'When you go home, tell them of us and say, "For your tomorrows these gave their today".'

[2] All manner of counter-factual scenarios have been painted over the years as to how the Germans might have reversed their fortunes on the Eastern front and once more turned their attention north. Ultimate victory was still three years and many more deaths away in 1942.

Britain was faced with a pitiless struggle that was far from over – was certainly a realistic one for the audience.

It was in that climate that the events giving rise to the detention of one Robert Liversidge came to pass. He was held without trial, under the notorious Regulation 18B; something no less than Winston Churchill later called 'in the highest degree odious'. But, if the life of the nation is at stake, as it was during the Second World War (and may be again, if extremists ever acquire sufficiently lethal weapons), can we afford the luxury of a full-scale trial with all the odds weighted towards the defence?

Liversidge, we know with hindsight, was not a traitor. But the person considered in the next essay in this part of the book, Georges Boudarel, certainly was – by his own admission. Yet he was able to take advantage of a substantial and intentional loophole in French justice to return to the country he had betrayed and resume a normal life.

We then consider a case concerning how those who (unlike Boudarel) gave their lives in honourable circumstances (*R (on the application of Fogg) v Secretary of State for Defence*), before finishing with two cases which raise another classic law and war question: to what extent should normal rules of civil liability apply to the armed forces?

The late Baroness Thatcher was a controversial figure, to say the least, but few could have disagreed when she pointed out around the turn of the century that health and safety concerns were 'essentially unsuited' to the armed forces. Gruff sergeant-majors shouting at young recruits and slumming on hard floors are the ordinary stuff of military training, however objectionable they might be in other contexts – to say nothing of working hours or handling dangerous equipment.

Two related questions arise in the cases considered. First, in the case of *Dennis and another v Ministry of Defence*, to what extent should ordinary citizens have to put up with their lives being interrupted by military exercises (in the case in question, fast jets disturbing a landowner's peace).

Secondly, in what became known as the 'Challenger claims', to what extent should the military escape liability for negligent actions in combat? In respect of the latter, it is well-established that decisions in the heat of battle should not lead to civilian law suits, or the armed forces would be hopelessly compromised. The appropriate consequence for negligent decisions would be for the military itself to remove the offending officer from command, and/or to conduct a court martial. But what exactly constitutes combat? And what of negative results flowing from incompetent decisions made well behind the lines or months before battle was joined? As we will see, the opinion of senior judges is divided on the point.

Traitors Imagined

In late August 1939, as German tanks were massing on the Polish border, the British Parliament hurriedly passed the Emergency Powers (Defence) Act 1939. The Act authorised the implementation of defence regulations which had been floating around in draft form throughout the inter-war period, awaiting what some correctly perceived to be the inevitable. The most stringent was Regulation 18B, which provided: 'If the Secretary of State has reasonable cause to believe any person to be of hostile origin or associations ... he may make an order against that person directing that he be detained.'

Enter Robert Liversidge, not a promising candidate for a Nazi fifth columnist, since, apart from anything else, he was Jewish. He volunteered for service with the armed forces in 1938, around the time Neville Chamberlain was promising peace in our time. After war broke out he started working in the RAF as an intelligence officer, and his subsequent problems seem to have arisen from his necessarily delicate work in that capacity. Early in 1940, MI5 had received intelligence about '*Jew swindlers*' using '*improper pressures ... in High Places*' to effect the release of some internees. Liversidge was arrested and charged with making a false statement. His flat was searched and the names of other persons known to the intelligence services were discovered. It also transpired that Liversidge was not his real name. The Secretary of State, John Anderson, authorised his detention.

Liversidge was able to appeal to an advisory board, but despite character references from the likes of Aneurin Bevan, he was unsuccessful. Thereafter he brought proceedings for false imprisonment against Anderson. He failed in the lower courts and appealed to the House of Lords.

The issue was straightforward. Regulation 18B empowered the Secretary of State to order the detention of someone if he had 'reasonable cause to believe' him to be of hostile associations. The question was whether it was only for him to judge what was reasonable, or if (upon a legal challenge by the detainee) the courts had jurisdiction to review the reasonableness of the belief.

The majority of the House of Lords chose the former: it was enough for Anderson to think what he thought about Liversidge. Lord Atkin, in his dissenting judgment, thought the opposite:

> I view with apprehension the attitude of judges who on a mere question of construction when face to face with claims involving the liberty of the subject show themselves more executive minded than the executive. ... In this country, amid the clash of arms, the laws are not silent. They may be changed, but they speak the same language in war as in peace. It has always been one of the pillars of freedom, one of the principles of liberty for which on recent authority we are now fighting, that the judges are no respecters of persons and stand between the subject and any attempted encroachments on his liberty by the executive, alert to see that any coercive action is justified in law. In this case I have listened to arguments which might have been addressed acceptably to the Court of King's Bench in the time of Charles I.
>
> I protest, even if I do it alone, against a strained construction put on words with the effect of giving an uncontrolled power of imprisonment to the minister ...

He went on to state that only Humpty Dumpty[3] could have construed the statute in line with the majority's decision.

As a matter of textual interpretation, Lord Atkin's judgment is unquestionably preferable to that of the majority. In any other context a requirement for a minister to have 'reasonable grounds' for some action would be justiciable; that is, someone with an interest in the outcome could challenge a decision on the basis that no such reasonable grounds existed. Since the war, that is the view that has prevailed, and the decision in *Liversidge v Anderson* has been gradually disowned by the courts.[4] It is

---

[3] A reference to the famous passage in *Through the Looking Glass*, when Humpty Dumpty claims that when he uses a word, it means what he wants it to mean, neither more nor less. I do not know if Lord Atkin was the first legal writer to invoke Lewis Carroll in this fashion, but he was assuredly not the last.

[4] See Lord Bingham of Cornhill, 'The Case of Liversidge v Anderson: the Rule of Law Amid the Clash of Arms', (2009) 43 *The International Lawyer*,

most unlikely that the majority's decision would be repeated in similar circumstances, and not simply because courts would be required to interpret the regulation in a manner most consistent with the European Convention on Human Rights.

And yet, is there something to be said in the other direction? The constitutional law expert Francis Bennion was one who did not support Lord Atkin's dissent. He reasoned[5] that 'the defence of liberty may imperatively require measures such as Regulation 18B in times of emergency, and the rule of law allows for this'.

Here is one of the great moral and legal dilemmas in wartime: there is no point in refusing to suspend or bend the rules if it means the enemy wins. If the Germans had prevailed then Britain would have been lumped with the Nazi Criminal Code, which required courts to interpret provisions in the manner *least* favourable to detainees.

All but the most optimistic would agree that there are some – however far-fetched – circumstances in which some fairly desperate suspension of the normal rules would be required, and Bennion may well be right that the rule of law (by any practical definition) allows for this.

The question therefore is whether those circumstances existed at the time of *Liversidge* justifying Regulation 18B. Even disregarding hindsight, it is not so clear that they did, for two reasons. First, Liversidge was let go very soon afterwards, and most of his fellow detainees were released well short of the war's conclusion. That suggests that the authorities did not actually fear them as much as they made out.[6]

Secondly, even allowing for the critical situation of the time, there were other options short of detention without trial. Something akin to the modern Special Immigration Appeals

---

pp 33–38.

[5] Letter to the *Denning Law Journal*, 1988.

[6] The same might be said, incidentally, for the detention of Americans of Japanese origin following Pearl Harbor, a drastic measure giving rise to the Supreme Court decision in *Korematsu v United States* 323 US 214 (1944). It was subsequently determined that the court was misled by the government in *Korematsu v United States* 584 F. Supp 1406 (1983). The absurdity of the situation there was made clear in *Ex parte Mitsuyi Endo* 323 US 283 (1944).

Commission (SIAC) might have been fashioned, under which suspected enemy aliens could have had independent counsel review classified material on their part. Whilst imperfect, SIAC is nevertheless superior to Regulation 18B in the way it protects the rights of detainees.

Perhaps if in modern times a 'dirty bomb' was found, or even used in Britain causing the deaths of tens of thousands, and there was compelling evidence that other such weapons were at large, it might justify some short-term extreme measures including detention without trial.[7] Absent such an imminent threat, however, experience teaches that the more the state has power to detain people the more it will go on to detain, and on ever flimsier grounds. *Liversidge* was wrongly decided then, and the lesson remains pertinent today.

[7]   Or even torture? The celebrated American lawyer and legal academic Alan Dershowitz argued in his book *Why Terrorism Works* (Yale University Press, 2002) that torture, if supported by an *ad hoc* judicial order, might be permitted where there is known to be a 'ticking bomb' hidden somewhere threatening the lives of thousands of innocent people.

Traitors Real

The first Indochina war (1946–1954), otherwise known as the French Vietnam War, was a notable event in 20th-century post-war colonial history. It was the first time in that period that a non-Western indigenous culture defeated a Western power in a conventional war. The decisive engagement came at the battle of Dien Bien Phu.

Arguably, Dien Bien Phu remains the only defeat of its kind: when France left Algeria, or America Vietnam (or Afghanistan and Iraq in more recent times), for example, neither was due to an outright defeat in the field, but rather because support at home for the continued expenditure of blood and treasure had evaporated.

As well as the historical significance, and amidst the inevitable carnage and horror, the French experience in Vietnam also contained its share of interesting human stories. One concerned the first two Americans to die in conflict in Vietnam: James 'Earthquake McGoon' McGovern[8] and his co-pilot Wallace Buford died the day before Dien Bien Phu fell, when the transport plane they were flying for a CIA front company assisting the French was shot down. Another concerned the grim aftermath of the war for the French prisoners. Decades after their ordeal they found that one of their chief tormentors, a traitor by the name of Georges Boudarel, was living amongst them in France itself. Unfortunately for the veterans, when seeking justice through the French and European courts, they were to find both law and justice trumped by realpolitik.

---

[8] McGovern's story is an intriguing one: a Second World War veteran, he fought in China under dubious circumstances in the Civil War which followed the Japanese defeat. He was captured but managed to bluff his way out. When his plane was hit above Dien Bien Phu, he managed to nurse it more than 70 miles towards Laos, but crashed just before reaching safety. His last words, heard over the radio, were to his co-pilot: 'Looks like this is it, son'. His remains were eventually recovered decades later and returned to the United States where he was reburied with military honours from both the United States and France.

Boudarel was a history professor in Saigon after the Second World War, where he led the Indochinese wing of the French Communist Party. In 1949 he was teaching philosophy, when he defected to the Viet Minh. They gave him the *nom de guerre* 'Dai Dong'.

After Dien Bien Phu, the French survivors were sent on forced marches through the jungle to prison camps run by sadistic guards, in a manner reminiscent of Japanese prison camps in the recently concluded Second World War. There they would have been shocked to find Boudarel working as a camp guard, giving brutal 'political re-education' lessons to his former fellow countrymen and dispensing cruelty *pour encourager les autres*. Thousands of prisoners died from hunger, disease or the harsh work and punishment regime of the camps.

Showing what seems to have been a distinct lack of self-awareness, Boudarel later returned to France, following the passage of a French law which gave a general amnesty to former deserters and other French citizens from the recent conflict.[9] Boudarel reassumed a teaching role and seems to have lived happily enough until, in 1991, his name was recognised by the veteran Wladyslaw Sobanski. Along with other veterans Sobanski began a class action seeking compensation for Boudarel's part in the prison abuses all those years earlier. Boudarel took a defensive stance, offering excuses on the lines that the guards had suffered from food shortages too, and blaming any failings he might have had on youthful ideological ignorance.

The action failed, both in the French domestic courts and finally the European Court of Human Rights, on the simple procedural ground that the 1966 Amnesty barred the claim, irrespective of the merits. Afterwards, some efforts were made by the disappointed veterans to obtain an exemption to the 1966 Amnesty in respect of crimes against humanity, but nothing came of it before Boudarel's death in 2003 at the age of 77. Justice, therefore, had first been delayed and then denied.

---

[9]   Law 66-409 of 18 June 1966. Doubtless the law was motivated in part by a wish not to repeat the terrible acts of reprisal that occurred in France post-liberation against real or imagined German collaborators.

The 1966 Amnesty has many parallels, including the Truth and Reconciliation Commission in post-Apartheid South Africa; the 'Lessons Learnt and Reconciliation Commission' in post-civil war Sri Lanka; and in Britain and Ireland recently with the tangled compromises that have formed part of the apparent conclusion of the Troubles in Northern Ireland.

In some of those instances, even convicted murderers have been released and admitted murderers have been told they will not face prosecution. All of those steps have occurred as part of a process of give and take between former protagonists in the bluntly utilitarian hope that any individual injustice will be outweighed by a lasting peace benefitting a greater number.

One is reminded of the masterful (if slightly ahistorical) speech by Christopher Reeve's American senator in the film version of *Remains of the Day*, in which he delivers a searing condemnation of his fellow country-house guests who have been trying to cut a deal with Nazi Germany. He warns that: 'The days when you could just act out of your noble instincts are over. Europe has become the arena of realpolitik; the politics of reality.'

It is the single word 'realpolitik' which perfectly encapsulates each brushing aside of individual injustices under the carpet found in all the examples in the preceding paragraph, as well as in Sobanski's failed case against Boudarel. Not for nothing did the lawyer Mark Freeman call his book on amnesties for mass atrocities *Necessary Evils*.[10]

The result of the case undoubtedly jarred with his former victims, but might be said to be in the nature of war. What is war, after all, but injustice writ large? And if a lesser form of injustice – that is to say, one not involving killing yet more people – is needed to bring a conflict to an end, then that has to be the lesser of two evils. Messy and tawdry compromises are never a comfort to the victims – but at least they should ensure that the number of victims is not increased.

---

[10] Mark Freeman, *Necessary Evils: Amnesties and the search for justice* (Cambridge University Press, 2009).

Respecting the Dead

Mention of naval battles in the Second World War tends to conjure up images of great capital ships trading murderous salvos of heavy shells, such as the *Bismarck* and the *Hood*, or great air assaults such as Taranto or Pearl Harbor. In reality, the most numerous participants in the war at sea were the rather less dramatic-looking ships of the Merchant Navy, undertaking the gruelling endurance tests in convoy seeing little of the enemy, dry land, or much else besides, though living all the while with the fear of attack sometime, somewhere. The intermittent bursts of terror occasioned by enemy action resulted in approximately 5,000 merchant ships being sunk with more than 30,000 hands lost.

That level of casualties strongly suggests that anyone who sailed under the Red Ensign (known to the sailors as the 'Red Duster', the flag of British merchant ships since 1674), should be considered to have been wartime participants the equal of their more glamorous counterparts in the Royal Navy's capital ships. But the case of *R (on the application of Fogg) v Secretary of State for Defence*[11] shows that not everyone agrees.

The case concerned the wreck of the cargo ship SS *Storaa*. She was assigned to traverse the English Channel, one of the most perilous of all Second World War voyages. Although the Channel ports were within easy reach of E-Boats and the Luftwaffe, the lack of comparable infrastructure left Britain with no choice but to use them when moving heavy equipment. The Germans mounted furious attempts to destroy them. Not for nothing did the Strait of Dover and the Wold Channel become known as 'Hell's Corner' and 'E-Boat Alley' respectively.

The crew of the *Storaa* would therefore have been under no illusions as to the risks when they set out on what was to be her last voyage, in late 1943. Four of those on board were Royal Navy gunners and three were Army gunners. Their weapons included a 12-pounder gun. The *Storaa* formed part of a convoy

---

[11]   [2006] EWCA Civ 1270.

of 19 ships, headed by HMS *Whitshed*, bound from Southend to Cardiff. On the night of 2/3 November, the convoy came under E-Boat attack and the *Storaa* returned fire in self-defence. After about ten minutes the *Storaa* was sunk with the loss of 22 lives. The official scroll commemorating the death of the chief officer recorded that he was 'one who served King and Country … and gave his life to save mankind from tyranny'.

Despite all that, upon the discovery of the wreck in the late 20th century, the Secretary of State for Defence stated that the *Storaa* had not been sunk 'while in military service' within the meaning of s 9(2) of the Military Remains Act 1986. Section 9(2) defined 'military service' as 'in service with, or being used for the purposes of, any of the armed forces …' The Secretary of State considered that only Royal Navy ships, or ships taken up by the Admiralty, could fall within that definition. On those grounds he refused to designate the wreck a war grave.

The daughters of a naval petty officer who had lost his life on board the *Storaa* brought proceedings for judicial review to challenge that decision. They succeeded in the High Court and the Secretary of State appealed to the Court of Appeal.

The Court of Appeal ruled that whether a vessel was 'in service with' any of the armed forces depended upon all the circumstances of the case, in particular the degree of control which the armed forces had over her at the particular time. In the case of the *Storaa*, the Admiralty had had control over whether she sailed in convoy; a Royal Navy vessel was in the convoy was to protect it; the master of the *Storaa* was obliged to obey the naval ship's commanding officer in all matters relating to navigation or security; the *Storaa* was armed and her guns were manned by military personnel; and at the time she was sunk she had been engaged in using her guns against the enemy. Therefore, the *Storaa* could properly be said to have been in military service at the relevant time. The appeal was accordingly dismissed and the wreck in due course was designated as a war grave under the Act.

It is true that not every grave of everyone who died in wartime should necessarily be considered a war grave. If the definition of war grave is extended too far then it will cease to have much meaning. There is accordingly a sound theoretical basis for s 9(2) of the 1986 Act. But the saga of the *Storaa* admitted only of one answer. Armed servicemen were on board who engaged the enemy when the expected – almost inevitable – attack came. 'Military service' is the only apt description of their actions at that point. It would be absurd if the gunners on board one of the naval escort ships were given one classification and those on board the *Storaa* another. Q-Ships were an integral part of the convoy strategy in countering U-Boats and E-Boats.

Perhaps the Secretary of State was treating the litigation as a test case, seeking general guidance, but the *Storaa* was not appropriate for that purpose because there was no serious dispute. Besides, the relatives of the *Storaa*'s victims should not have had to foot the bill for the courts to settle the law. The right answer was given in the case, but the question should never have been asked.

A Flying Nuisance

I have a friend who grew up in the 1970s near RAF Waddington, where Vulcan bombers were based. He has dryly remarked on more than one occasion that those who complain about noise from Heathrow should try having a few sets of four Olympus engines in a holding pattern above their house every other afternoon.

Admittedly that is less than convincing as a moral argument: rather like suggesting those who have lost one leg should not complain since others might have lost two. But it is still true that the Vulcan hails from a very different age. It first flew in 1952, when the British jet industry was in its heyday. That year a disastrous crash of a DH 110 Sea Vixen at the Farnborough Air Show left 29 spectators and two crew members dead. Not only did none of the survivors or the families of the deceased sue anyone afterwards, the organisers did not even stop the event. Instead the dead bodies were cordoned off and the rest of the day's activities proceeded with a mildly adjusted schedule.

No doubt the primary reason was that all adults present had lived through the war, and would therefore have experienced even worse tragedies on many occasions. They were, by necessity, a more stoic lot in those days. Nor was the Farnborough incident simply an example of peculiarly British stiff-upper-lip: there was an even worse accident at Le Mans three years later, but again the organisers did not stop the event.

In more recent times, by contrast, the European Court of Human Rights has had to grapple with the Heathrow denizens bringing proceedings about aircraft making them lose sleep. The claim was rejected, though not without a few newspaper columnists dispensing insults about pointless claims and an enfeebled age.

In the case of *Dennis and another v Ministry of Defence*,[12] the claimant was rather more successful. Dennis was the owner of a stately home in Norfolk. He brought an action against the

---

[12]   [2003] All ER (D) 300 (Apr).

Ministry of Defence arising from the loss of amenity caused by Harrier jets flying from RAF Wittering. The claim was brought in common law nuisance and for breaches of Art 8 (the right to privacy) of and Art 1 of the First Protocol (the right to property) to the European Convention on Human Rights. Despite making the claim, Dennis was anxious that the judge accept that he was a supporter of the RAF and that he strongly believed in the need for a fast jet force – just not in his backyard.

If it had been a purely civilian matter, he could simply have sued for nuisance and it is hard to imagine that any private activity which generated a noise equivalent to a low-flying fast jet would not result in the perpetrator either being compelled to stop or to pay substantial damages or both.

Where the military is concerned, however, there is a strong countervailing factor in the form of the public interest in maintaining an effective defence force. That means, among other things, regularly flying fast jets for training and patrols, and obviously the planes have to fly somewhere. In a small and relatively crowded country like the United Kingdom the chances of them always avoiding civilian areas are slim.

Moreover, tight controls about speed and altitude are properly imposed on civilian pilots, but fighter pilots have to hone their skills flying as low and as fast as possible. One Welsh farmer in the 1970s adopted the more imaginative approach of painting 'Piss Off Biggles' on the roof of a barn; the RAF thereafter used the message as a navigational reference point, while respecting the farmer's wishes to some extent by flying slightly higher.

The approach the judge took in Dennis's case was that while the public interest should be considered in relation to nuisance, selected individuals should not be forced to bear the cost of the public benefit. It was therefore appropriate to weigh the public interest not when deciding whether a nuisance existed, but at the remedy stage. That way, it would be open to the court to allow the nuisance to continue while requiring the public as opposed to Dennis alone to pay for its benefit. Accordingly, Dennis could be compensated in monetary terms but the RAF would not be prevented from continuing flying.

In the event the damages were assessed at £950,000. The flying continued until the Harrier fleet was retired in somewhat controversial circumstances (the remaining aircraft were sold at a knock-down price to a grateful United States Marine Corps).

For all of the changing times, Dennis's case remains a good example of the traditional application of the common law and of how the public interest can be preserved without eviscerating the claimant's private rights. There is no justification for the military to have *carte blanche* to fly anywhere it likes in peacetime: Britain is not, after all, a military dictatorship. Moreover, the fundamental importance of property rights – which remain one of the keys to freedom and economic prosperity – requires that when the state does something which reduces the value of a citizen's property, the citizen should be compensated, even if there is a strong public interest in the state's activity.

Some hardened RAF veterans might be unimpressed. Even in the halcyon days of the British jet age, however, fairly strict controls were imposed by the RAF itself on flying over residential areas. Also, they might even see an upside. Flight Lieutenant Alan Pollock's legendary protest by way of flying *through* Tower Bridge in a Hawker Hunter jet[13] was, I suspect, all the more satisfying for him knowing how many regulations he must have been breaking while he was doing it.

---

[13] Both the Farnborough crash and Pollock's protest are memorably described in James Hamilton-Paterson's *Empire of the Clouds: When Britain's Aircraft Ruled the World* (Faber & Faber, 2010).

The Challenger Claims

The Prussian General Moltke the Elder once said that no plan survives contact with the enemy. Real life has confirmed that aphorism on countless occasions: rare it is that individual battles, let alone entire wars, have ever gone to plan. Even in the most successful engagements there have almost always been needless casualties caused by equipment failure, human error or a combination thereof. In both Gulf Wars, for example, despite the overwhelming superiority of coalition forces, the high level of technology at their disposal, and the swift conclusion of the initial military operations with extraordinarily low allied casualties, there were still friendly fire incidents ('Blue on Blue' in British military parlance) where British and American soldiers were killed by their own side due to mistaken identity.

Because of the inevitable consequences of the 'fog of war' and the undesirability of civilian judges trying to sift through the evidence long after the event, the common law has developed the doctrine of 'combat immunity', under which anything that happens during battle cannot be challenged in the courts (or, in legal terms, is non-justiciable).[14]

In *Mulcahy v Ministry of Defence*,[15] the Court of Appeal preferred to see combat immunity not so much as an entirely separate principle as the result of a general conclusion that it was not fair, just or reasonable to regard the Crown or its martial emanations as under a duty of care to avoid injury or death in their acts or omissions in the conduct of an active military operation or act of war, but we can leave aside such doctrinal niceties for now.

In the 2010s, the families of victims of one friendly fire incident in the 2003 Iraq War brought proceedings against the Ministry of Defence (MOD). The MOD applied to strike out the claims on the ground of combat immunity. The Supreme Court by a majority decision ruled against the MOD on that preliminary

[14] See for example *Shaw Savill & Albion Co Ltd v Commonwealth, ex p Marais* (1940) 66 CLR 344.
[15] [1996] QB 732.

issue and allowed the claims to proceed to trial.[16] There were claims arising out of different incidents, but I shall confine myself to what were called the 'Challenger claims'. In my view the dissenting judgment of Lord Mance was compelling, while the decision of the majority was unsupportable in principle and might have serious adverse consequences for future deployments.

The Challenger claims involved one British Challenger II tank firing on another, with fatal consequences. The claimants alleged that if the tanks had been properly equipped with existing technology and equipment, the incident would have been prevented.

The majority of the Supreme Court accepted that combat immunity was not limited to the presence of the enemy or the occasions when contact with the enemy had been established. It extended to all active operations against the enemy in which service personnel were exposed to attack, including the planning and preparation for the operations in which the armed forces might come under attack or meet armed resistance. Further, there was no duty, in battle conditions, to maintain a safe system of work.

The majority accepted that the doctrine should be narrowly construed. It extended to the planning of and preparation for military operations in which injury had been sustained. But it did not extend to the planning and preparation, in general, for possible unidentified further operations.[17]

With respect to the Challenger claims, at the stage when men were being trained, whether pre-deployment or in theatre, or decisions were being made about the fitting of equipment to tanks or other fighting vehicles, there was time to think things through, to plan and to exercise judgment. Those activities were sufficiently far removed from the pressures and risks of active operations against the enemy for it not to be unreasonable to expect a duty of care to be exercised, as long as the standard of

---

[16] *Smith and others v Ministry of Defence* [2013] UKSC 41.
[17] See Lord Hope at [88], [92] and [98] of the judgment.

care that was imposed had regard to the nature of those activities and to their circumstances.

Recognising some dangerous implications, Lord Hope cautioned:

> [I]t is of paramount importance that the work that the armed services do in the national interest should not be impeded by having to prepare for or conduct active operations against the enemy under the threat of litigation if things should go wrong. The court must be especially careful, in their case, to have regard to the public interest, to the unpredictable nature of armed conflict and to the inevitable risks that it gives rise to when it is striking the balance as to what is fair, just and reasonable.

And yet, by allowing the case to proceed to trial, it seems to me that Lord Hope did not take proper account of that paramount importance.

The decision of the majority relies on the following argument. A casualty might occur due to an equipment problem foreseeable and entirely within the power of the MOD to remedy before long before the war had started or even looked like starting. If so, why should the MOD hide behind combat immunity for decisions taken thousands of miles away and many months before hostilities?

The answer was set out in cutting fashion by Lord Mance. The supply of technology and equipment, training for active services, and decisions taken on the ground during an action are all inevitably inter-linked. The claimants had been careful not to make any criticism of the commanders on the ground. But the attribution of responsibility could not depend on how the claimant framed his case. Lord Hope recognised the problem but considered that all such circumstances had to be evaluated with a view to striking a balance between competing considerations. Lord Mance concluded the opposite – that all such circumstances were inter-related and essentially non-justiciable.

At para [131] he stated:

> The claimants' case is that during or after any war any injured soldier or the relatives or dependants of any soldier killed in

combat could sue the state for alleged failures in the preparation or equipping of the armed forces for combat. Logically, if that is so, then a soldier might, even during the war, complain that his or her equipment or training was inadequate and that it would be a breach of the state's common law duty of care and/or duties under the Human Rights Convention even to order him or her to go into combat with it. If domestic legislation compelled this, then the soldier could seek relief in the Strasbourg court – maybe even interim relief prohibiting the further use or giving of orders to use the allegedly defective equipment. (…) Pointing to defective equipment and seeking to ban its use could have a considerable disruptive effect. Not only would there be a huge potential diversion of time and effort in litigation of such issues in an area of essential national interest (whether before, during or after hostilities). There must be risks that the threat of exhaustive civil litigation following any active military operation would affect decision-making and lead to a defensive approach, both at the general procurement and strategic stages and at the tactical and combat stages when equipment was being deployed.

By way of example he cited a number of well-known incidents – the defeat at Isandlwana, the failure of the War Office to appreciate Lancelot de Mole's idea for the tank in 1912 and the fall of Singapore.

As the barrister Adam Wagner pointed out when I first wrote about the case, it calls to mind the old rhyme:

> For want of a nail the shoe was lost.
> For want of a shoe the horse was lost.
> For want of a horse the rider was lost.
> For want of a rider the message was lost.
> For want of a message the battle was lost.
> For want of a battle the kingdom was lost.
> And all for the want of a horseshoe nail.

In short, issues arising from tactical decisions are for military debriefing sessions and, where appropriate, courts martial. Procurement issues are for the political process. Neither is suitable for the civilian courtrooms.

Afterword

When I first published a version of the above,[18] I received a detailed, intelligent reply by someone who was obviously very familiar with the armed forces. His argument in essence was that the army had a long and undistinguished history in trying to get away with ill-treatment of soldiers and generally unmeritorious behaviour by claiming that it was entitled to do things the general population could not. I can see the force of the argument, but then again, another episode after I first wrote the article was the Al-Sweady Inquiry, which showed that a number of sustained attacks on the British armed forces in Iraq were wholly made up nonsense, brought by Britain's enemies as a form of 'lawfare', to undermine British morale and force changes that would harm operational efficiency.[19]

Drawing the line between law and war is never easy. Lest it be thought I am against properly holding to account those who fail the troops in the field, here is a letter I had published in *The Times* on 23 September 2013. It was the lead letter for the day:

Dear Sir

George Webster correctly applauds Paul Flynn MP's defence of the generals of the Great War against the common misconception of 'Lions led by Donkeys' (letter, Sept 20). Contrary to popular belief, the phrase did not originate in that conflict. More to the point, had British generals been hopelessly incompetent it is unlikely that they would have finished on the winning side, never mind with the victories of the 'hundred days' in 1918 behind them. In fact, 1918 was probably the only time in its entire history that the British army could claim to be the most powerful field army in the world.

There, is, however, one point on which I would take issue with Mr Flynn. It is true that few ministers have covered themselves in glory with respect to defence in recent years, whether in terms of short-term procurement, long-view White Papers or, most importantly, starting and conducting foreign wars. But

---

[18] On my blog 'A Lawyer Writes': http://timesandotherthings.blogspot. co.uk/2013/06/smith-and-others-v-ministry-of-defence.html.

[19] See https://www.gov.uk/government/publications/al-sweady-inquiry-report.

it is another matter to exculpate today's generals for any of those issues. Where is the evidence that any senior officers advised the government in 2003 that the British army was wholly unsuited in terms of training, equipment and rules of engagement for the reconstruction and counter-insurgency that would have to follow any successful invasion of Iraq? How many officers have had their careers halted by the subsequent events in that country or Afghanistan?

Instead the armed forces have successfully inferred that it has all been the fault of politicians, without mentioning who advises those politicians. This is no more honourable than those former members of Mr Blair's cabinet who claimed in their later memoirs that they did not really support the Iraq War and had doubts about the PM's judgement, despite not voting against the invasion or resigning their posts at the time.

Meanwhile, another letter to *The Times* was published on 7 April 2015, by five former Chiefs of Defence Staff. It stated that 'Recent legislation and judicial findings have extended the domestic law of negligence to the combat zone, where civilian norms of duty of care cannot apply. The increased risk of prosecution constrains the ability of commanders to respond to fast-moving situations on the battlefield. This could lead to a generation of risk-averse military leaders, which undermines the world-class status of our armed forces.'

The letter went on to urge the government to 'recognise the primacy of the Geneva Conventions in war by derogating from the European Convention on Human Rights in time of war and redefining combat immunity'.

The key point is in the letter's final sentence: 'The military is neither above nor exempt from the law, but war demands different norms and laws than the rest of human activity'.

Part V: Religion and the Law

INTRODUCTION

(1) Everyone has the right to freedom of thought, conscience and religion; this right includes freedom to change his religion or belief and freedom, either alone or in community with others and in public or private, to manifest his religion or belief, in worship, teaching, practice and observance.

(2) Freedom to manifest one's religion or beliefs shall be subject only to such limitations as are prescribed by law and are necessary in a democratic society in the interests of public safety, for the protection of public order, health or morals, or for the protection of the rights and freedoms of others.

Article 9 of the European Convention on Human Rights

Religion and the law has evolved to become one of the most fascinating moral, philosophical and legal questions of our age, particularly since the Human Rights Act 1998 came into force, giving citizens the right to bring claims for alleged breaches of Convention rights in domestic courts.

For the most part, cases involving religion concern clashes of rights: someone contending that their religious beliefs justify some sort of exemption to the general law which applies to everyone else. This requires the courts to reconcile Art 9(1) and (2) as set out above. We will see several examples in this part and analogous issues elsewhere in the book as well. The first case concerns the now defunct crime of blasphemy, a hangover from the days in which the church was at the centre of both public and private lives. Blasphemy is, in my view, a paradigm example of a flawed law; treating one set of beliefs ahead of others for no good reasons. Beliefs, religious or otherwise, do not deserve or even require the law's protection.

The second case concerns whether there should be any restriction on people holding high office at the same time as holy orders; once again, my argument is that they should all be treated equally; in this case, my demand that religion not be treated separately works to the advantage of the religious.

'As every schoolboy knows', said Chancellor Hill in the third case in this part, 'King Harold was killed at the Battle of Hastings by an arrow through the eye.' Sadly I doubt so many schoolboys know this nowadays. Those who do may be wrong in any event: the sources (including the Bayeaux Tapestry) are ambiguous. The true nature of Harold's death will therefore always remain, in the words of Donald Rumsfeld, a 'known unknown'.

Another 'known unknown' for Harold concerns where he was buried. That uncertainty gave rise to the case discussed in the chapter, where a group of churchwardens sought permission to carry out an excavation in the hope of finding his grave. Most think Harold lies in Waltham Abbey, though no likely grave has ever been found there, despite a number of excavations over the years. Sadly, the alternative theory turned out to be thinner than the Saxon ranks after Harold's death.

I nevertheless retain a touch of regret that the excavation did not take place. I would not have objected had I been the owner of the land, because I would not be inclined to be sentimental about any dead body, let alone a body almost 1,000 years old. But the land in question was owned by a church and the church was entitled to act according to its beliefs, encapsulated here in the ecclesiastical law that imposed strict conditions on interfering with graves.

We then turn to some more 'clash of rights' cases. Here some basic principles need to be established, which have a substantial overlap with other rights and freedoms. Freedom of speech and freedom of religion require the state to allow people to express their views and undertake their own religious ceremonies without restraint, so long as they do not expect anyone else to pay for those views or to have contrary views silenced. But neither right requires anyone's beliefs to be recognised by the state – either in terms of funding or in terms of influencing important public decisions or in terms of special protection against criticism or ridicule.

Blasphemy!

In the early to mid-2000s, a play called *Jerry Springer: the Opera* was performed in various parts of the United Kingdom as well as being broadcast on the BBC. The work was a parody of Springer's well-known television chat show. The play, set to music, consisted of two parts. The first was a direct lampooning of the television show, ending with the host being murdered. The second revolved around the host imagining his descent into Hell, where the first act characters reappeared as Satan, Christ, God, Mary and Adam and Eve, most of whom were portrayed very unflatteringly. The host treated them as his chat show guests and offered some farcical mediation between their historic differences.

The point of the production was to send up the abysmally bad taste of Springer's show and the squalid lives of the usual sort of guests.

It was also no doubt intended to be funny, though one Mr Green, who belonged to a group called 'Christian Voice', was not amused. He accepted that the primary target of the play was Springer and his lowbrow programme, not the Christian religion. Nevertheless, he sought to bring a private prosecution for blasphemous libel in respect of the play.

Green's case was that, no matter what the merits or demerits of the artistic qualities of the play, it contained material which was contemptuous and reviling of the Christian religion, of Christ and several other biblical characters, and of the tenets of the Church. He argued further that the play was delivered in a scurrilous and ludicrous manner. As such, he contended, the play amounted to the offence of criminal blasphemous libel, whether or not its principal target was Springer.

The district judge refused to issue the summonses, because the intended prosecution was barred by the Theatres Act 1968.[1]

---

[1]   Section 2(4)(a) of the Theatres Act 1968, which states: '(4) No person shall be proceeded against in respect of a performance of a play or anything said or done in the course of a performance — (a) for an offence at common law where it is of the essence of the offence that the performance or, as the case

But she held in any event that there was no case of blasphemous libel. Green applied to challenge that decision in the High Court by way of judicial review. In December 2007 his challenge was dismissed.[2]

Most felt that the litigation amounted to the end of the road for the offence of blasphemy as well. Green's solicitor was not happy about that. In *The Times* of 5 March 2008 he wrote:

> The last blasphemy case was brought 30 years ago and it would appear as though the Establishment of this country has moved a long way since then. Many believe that the law is an anachronism which has no place in a modern Britain. We believe that the contrary is true.
>
> Recently there has been another blasphemy case which we believe has fallen foul of the law, namely the grotesque statue of Jesus Christ with an erect penis in the Baltic Art Centre, Gateshead. Many Christians demonstrated against this and the strength of feeling ran high. Many expressed their desire to destroy the statue, but desisted, knowing this not to be lawful. Those same people have expressed a desire to assist in a private prosecution for blasphemy. The police have shown no interest in dealing with these grievances, as far as we are aware, and the art centre displayed the statue until the end of the exhibition. We strongly believe that it is in the public interest to prevent such lewd and offensive displays.
>
> It would seem that because Christians are peace-loving their faith is now considered fair game by the liberal Establishment and arts world. The law which is in place to protect that which is central to millions of people in Britain (15 per cent of whom regularly go to church) will offer no redress against gratuitous offence against God and their faith. With only three prosecutions in 100 years, it can hardly be said that the law has a chilling effect on free speech. Indeed, Richard Dawkins has never been threatened with a blasphemy prosecution. The law is there to stop only the most outrageous, spiteful, gratuitous

---

may be, what was said or done was obscene, indecent, offensive, disgusting or injurious to morality.' Similar wording in the Broadcasting Act 1990 precluded the prosecution being brought in respect of the BBC's televising of the play.

[2] See *R (on the application of Green) v City of Westminster Magistrates' Court and others* [2007] EWHC 2785 (Admin). In March 2008 the House of Lords refused permission to appeal that decision.

> acts which serve no legitimate aim in a democratic society, other than to insult the Christian faith.

With respect, the author was trying to have it both ways. On the one hand, he claimed that the law could hardly have a chilling effect on free speech, given that only three prosecutions had been brought in 100 years; on the other hand, he wished that it was used more often.

He then sought to justify the law on the basis that 'millions' of British are Christian. But he did not cite the views of those millions on whether or not they felt the need of the criminal law to protect their faith from bad taste jokes or satire, or as he put it '*redress against gratuitous offence against God and their faith*'.

The short answer is that I am fairly sure that God Himself can shake off any gratuitous offence, and his followers ought to be able to do the same. There are many things which every person of any faith – or no faith – might personally find offensive, but it is not at all clear that the criminal law should try and intervene.

The number of British people who are Christians does not settle the argument either: other faiths are catching up with Christianity in terms of numbers, and may in a few years' time surpass it. They too would want the protection of the criminal law if it is afforded to Christians. And the obvious problem is that what is sacred to one religion is blasphemy to another – which is one reason why we have had so much religious conflict over the years.

The article was a classic attempt to justify incursions into freedom of speech: classify the impugned work as not contributing to a 'legitimate aim in a democratic society' (to use the wording of the European Convention on Human Rights), or say that it 'distorts' debate.

The classic response is to point out that it is not art which has to prove that it serves a legitimate aim in a democratic society. It is *restrictions* on art which have to prove that they serve a legitimate aim in a democratic society, and that they are proportionate to that aim. Banning *Jerry Springer: the Opera* serves no purpose: if someone does not wish to see it, they have no need to buy a ticket. Or, if it is on television, offended viewers can change the channel.

The same answer should have been given in a robust fashion to the Sikh protestors who staged a violent demonstration about *Behzti* ('Dishonour' in Punjabi), a Sikh play with which they happened to disagree. Once again the protestors appeared to have no clue about freedom of expression – and in that case one could argue that the play in question was making a much more important point (about oppression of women within the Sikh faith) than simply poking fun at Springer and his tasteless show.[3]

It comes back to three fundamental principles: one law for all, freedom of speech, and a separation of church and state. And that means no blasphemy laws.

Afterword

It was indeed the end of the road for blasphemy laws not so long afterwards. The common law offences of blasphemy and blasphemous libel were abolished by the Criminal Justice and Immigration Act 2008.

The origin of its abolition, aside from the observed dearth of successful prosecutions, was a select committee appointed in May 2002 by the House of Lords 'to consider and report on the law relating to religious offences'. In April 2003 the committee reported that it could find no consensus on whether a new law against blasphemy was required, but concluded that if there was a law it should apply to all faiths and not just Christianity. The eventual response of the Commons was the Racial and Religious Hatred Act 2006. At the time of its introduction the Home Secretary, David Blunkett, suggested the blasphemy laws might be repealed after the 2006 Act came into force.

I have attacked the 2006 Act before.[4] Attempts to criminalise abuse of religion inevitably constitute – despite the apparent

---

[3]   *Behzti* was written by Gurpreet Kaur Bhatti. Violent protests took place in late 2004 when the play was performed in the United Kingdom. Those objecting pointed to a scene set in a Gurdwara of rape, physical abuse and murder.

[4]   See *Cases, Causes and Controversies*, Chapter 39.

paradox – an unwarranted restriction on freedom of religion, not to say freedom of speech. Good intentions – which no doubt lay behind the Act – rarely cure bad legislation.

Holy Orders and High Office

Rotten boroughs were one of the most rotten aspects of the generally rotten electoral system of centuries past. They were parliamentary constituencies with small enough populations for the landowner to bribe the voters or threaten them with eviction if they did not vote for him (easily ascertainable in those days as there was no secret ballot). They remained a blight on the political landscape until the Reform Act of 1832, a measure supported by the then-Prime Minister, Earl Grey of tea fame, and opposed by a former Prime Minister, the Duke of Wellington of Waterloo fame.

One particularly rotten borough was the Tolkienesque-sounding Old Sarum in Wiltshire. In 1801 it was responsible for a political controversy involving the equally Tolkienesque-sounding John Horne Took. The controversy led to an example of political blight which is unfortunately still with us, namely *ad hoc* legislation which remains in force long after the problem it was designed to address has vanished. In this case the *ad hoc* measure lasted for two centuries, before being abolished not because of principle but because another set of transient circumstances had arisen which obstructed the ruling party of the day. The sorry saga is a lesson in how poorly the rule of law has been understood by lawmakers throughout history.

Took had an interesting life before entering Parliament. He once spent a year in prison for his part in signing an advertisement soliciting subscriptions for the relief of the relatives of the Americans 'murdered by the King's troops at Lexington and Concord' during the American Revolutionary War.

Prior to 1801 he had tried and failed to become elected in a normal constituency, but found his way into Parliament by gaining control of Old Sarum. His election was opposed by Lord Temple, brother in law of William Pitt. Temple objected to the fact that Took had taken Holy Orders. Thanks in part to his efforts the House of Commons (Clergy Disqualification) Act 1801 was passed, which debarred any future priest from election to the House of Commons.

No one did anything about the Act until 2001, when the incumbent Labour government suddenly found the Act was obstructing the appointment of their prospective candidate David Cairns, who was a laicised Catholic priest. Labour hurriedly cobbled together a bill to amend the Act.

Once again, therefore, constitutional change was being proposed not for principled reasons but simply because of one individual who happened to be in or out of favour with the ruling party of the day.

The Act of 1801 was unprincipled for two reasons. First, the suitability of any particular parliamentary candidate is a matter not for *ad hoc* legislation but for the voters. If they want someone who has one (or ten) other jobs then they should be entitled to have him (or her). Secondly, legislation should not be for *ad hoc* political convenience. The rule of law requires that legislation should be general and abstract, not tailored to any particular groups or institutions.

Regrettably, though perhaps not unsurprisingly, the honourable members did not discuss constitutional fundamentals. Instead they offered personal anecdotes and, in the case of the Tories, took pot shots about the timing of the proposed legislation. Anne Widdecombe, for example, offered:

> I do not believe that being a Member of Parliament is compatible with the priestly vocation ... I do not believe that a Member of Parliament could represent constituents adequately while continuing to serve as a full-time priest, or that a priest could administer to his flock adequately while undertaking duties as a full-time Member of Parliament.

That might or might not be true for the priestly or any other vocation, but once again it should have been a matter for the voters, not Widdecombe's anecdotal claims. Perhaps there are candidates who would be all the better for doing both jobs, and thus not beholden to the party whip for their future income prospects. The rise of the professional political class, an ever-expanding group of people who have done nothing since university beyond working in politics, journalism or PR, is one of the blights of the modern age. Many might prefer to have an MP with experience of earning a living in the uncompromising world of the private sector than one who had been nothing but a researcher, a speechwriter and an MP.[5]

Still, it is possible to bring about the right result for the wrong reason, and this Parliament managed with the House of Commons (Removal of Clergy Disqualification) Act 2001.

Reflecting its unprincipled origin, the Act did not do away with all constitutional anomalies, since it made provision for the continuing disqualification of any bishop sitting in the House of Lords as a Lord Spiritual. It should not be necessary to point out that constitutional principle would demand removal of the bishops from the Lords, rather than carving out yet more exceptions in breach of the rule of law. It will not be long before other religious groups demand parity, and it is a safe bet they will not ask for it by way of removing the Anglican exception but rather demanding the same privilege for themselves, and thus breaching the rule of law more rather than less.

---

[5]   This point arises again later in the book, as a partial explanation for the unsatisfactory state of present-day employment law.

1066 and All That

Many headlines appeared early in February 2013 as a body found under a carpark in Leicester was confirmed, following DNA testing, carbon dating and examination of documentary evidence, to be that of Richard III.[6]

It was the sort of coup of which all archaeologists and historians dream. The most highly prized coup is one which overturns received wisdom about a well-known historical event, such as the historian John Grehan attempted, also in early 2013, with his book arguing that the Battle of Hastings did not take place on Senlac Ridge after all, but instead a mile away at Caldbec Hill.[7]

Grehan's theory has some circumstantial evidence in support, but unless someone digs up 10,000 bodies together with a lot of arrowheads and other battlefield detritus in the vicinity, it is likely to remain no more than conjecture. For what it is worth, it seems to me rather more plausible than another alternative site, on modern-day Crowhurst, advanced by a local historian, Nick Austin.

Earlier this century, a similarly optimistic claim was made about the fate of the body of the battle's most famous victim. In 2003 the incumbents and churchwardens of the parish of Holy Trinity, Bosham, formed the view that the body of Harold Godwinson himself might lie beneath their church. If true, that would be a worthy coup to say the least: Harold's defeat on that bloody October day was probably the single most significant event in English history, and after Richard III's discovery he is now the only monarch since Edward the Confessor whose place of burial is unknown.

[6] Of course we cannot know for certain that the body was that of Richard. But, applying something akin to the legal test of the balance of probability, it seems more likely that the body was that of Richard than anyone else. In fact most experts at the time of writing seemed to think there was no reasonable doubt on the matter.

[7] John Grehan and Martin Mace, *The Battle of Hastings 1066 – The Uncomfortable Truth* (Pen & Sword Books, 2012).

The Bosham hopefuls therefore petitioned the Consistory Court for the necessary 'faculty' for the archaeological investigation of two gravesites in the nave of their church. They wished to open a coffin and remove a sample of bone for carbon dating testing and destructive DNA testing. The petition was heard by Chancellor Hill, whose decision was given later the same year.[8]

The relevant ecclesiastical law was (and remains) based on the Christian doctrine that burial in consecrated land is final and permanent. That doctrine creates a strong presumption against any disturbance of human remains. In order for it to be overturned it is necessary to show 'a cogent and compelling case for the legitimacy of any research.'

Though a contrary view was expressed during the proceedings, Chancellor Hill accepted that the possibility of finding Harold's final resting place would pass the test – an obvious and gladdening conclusion given Harold's historical significance.

The potential importance of an investigation is not sufficient, however, as it also has to have a realistic chance of success, and it was for that reason that the Bosham petition failed.

The petitioners relied on a variety of accounts, beginning with the depiction in the Bayeaux Tapestry of Harold's visit to 'Bosham Ecclesia' in 1064. They also referred to excavations in 1865 which exposed a tomb of a child reputed to be the daughter of King Canute, and the opening in 1954 of a tomb which might have contained Harold's bones.

The problem was that all that evidence was rather fanciful, to say the least. One assumes there would not be much left of Harold's body after more than nine centuries. Whether by arrow or not, his death was certainly very bloody: legend has it that only his consort, Edith Swannesha, was able to identify his body after the battle. No skull was found in the 1954 excavation, so it might have been a body killed in battle (or the subject of later vandalism), but the bones were considered by experts to belong to a man older than Harold was at the time of his death. More

---

[8]   *Re Holy Trinity, Bosham* [2004] 2 All ER 820.

to the point, most surviving evidence points to Harold being buried at Waltham Abbey, even though no plausible grave has ever been found there.

Then there was the low probability that DNA testing or carbon dating would accomplish anything. The prospect of recovering Y-chromosome material from any bone material was considered to be only 10%–30%, and in any event Harold had no identifiable living descendants with whom any results could be compared (those offered by the petitioners had claims which were, to put it politely, inconclusive). Carbon dating was thought to have too wide a margin of error. The petition was therefore dismissed and the remains left undisturbed.

The outcome was probably inevitable, given the weight of the evidence. It has to follow that, legally speaking, the petition was ill-advised. Then again, who with any historical curiosity could fail to be intrigued by the notion that Harold's body might be discovered, providing a direct link to what I have already described as probably the most influential single day in the country's history? The Battle of Hastings deserves that title for many reasons: aside from rewriting land law and imposing his own aristocracy, without William's intervention the modern English language would have been very different. I therefore retain a tinge of regret that no investigation was undertaken, though one has to respect the right of the church to apply ecclesiastical law with regard to its own premises.

The discovery of Richard III will doubtless encourage the remaining Bosham faithful. But the chances of a positive identification of Richard were always much higher than Harold, since it was known that Richard was buried in Leicester, and unlike Harold he had identifiable descendants with whom any DNA could be compared. I suspect that his discovery might also revive the theory about Edward IV being illegitimate – though most consider that to be no more than another wishful theory advanced by historians seeking their own place in history.

Afterword

Perhaps inevitably, some litigation followed about Richard III too, concerning where he should be reburied. The case was *R (on the application of The Plantagenet Alliance Ltd) v Secretary of State for Justice and others*.[9] Although there was some interesting historical material in the judgment, most of the controversy concerned whether the claim should have been brought at all, given that it was not to determine the reburial site, but rather to argue over who should make the decision, which some felt was a pointless piece of lawyer's pedantry.[10]

Meanwhile, since this article was first published, an excavation of both Senlac Ridge and Caldbec Hill was undertaken by Channel 4's *Time Team* programme. It failed to find any archaeological evidence of the battle at either site, though the dig was apparently not very extensive at the former. The programme also investigated but dismissed Crowhurst due to a lack of supporting evidence.

Using ground-penetrating radar to survey the land as it would have been in 1066, the filmmakers concluded that the battle would have taken place very near Senlac Ridge, but from a different direction.

It was a moderate conclusion that seemed plausible, but unfortunately their proposed site was under roads and housing and thus it was not possible to carry out an excavation. It did seem to me though that the question of what the terrain was at the time – assuming it is possible to tell accurately – would be of significance. The Normans, wearing heavy armour, would not have formed up in a marshy area (as apparently the base of Senlac Ridge was at the time). Nor would the English have voluntarily formed a shield wall on a gentle slope; they would have preferred the steepest possible to negate the Norman cavalry. A narrow isthmus in the marshland would have been Harold's logical choice, to prevent flanking manoeuvres by the Normans and as part of his general strategy of preventing a breakout by the Normans. If he secured such a site, it would also explain why the battle lasted much longer than most mediaeval

---

[9] [2014] EWHC 1662 (QB).
[10] See D. Hart, 'Richard III: fairness and public interest litigation', *UK Human Rights Blog*, 28 May 2014, http://ukhumanrightsblog. com/2014/05/28/richard-iii-fairness-and-public-interest-litigation/.

battles, which usually turned into a rout within an hour or so when one side gained the upper hand. If Harold only had a small area to defend, his shield wall would have taken much longer to break. But, pending a major archaeological find, the site of the battle will forever remain the subject of speculation.[11]

[11] Published in the *New Law Journal*, vol 163, 8 February 2013, p 142.

Religion and Foster Parents

An interesting case[12] emerged early in the 2010s concerning a Christian couple who wished to become foster parents. They were open about the fact that their religious teachings shunned homosexuality. The local authority indicated that it had some difficulty with this, because their guidelines banned any discrimination on the ground of sexual orientation. Could it be right, the press and the public naturally asked, that a couple's religious views might preclude them from becoming foster parents, if in every other respect they would be model candidates?

The first question – not considered anywhere much in the literature – is whether or not the same test should apply for placing children with foster parents as for removing children from their original parents.

If the test were to be the same, then it would have to be far less intrusive than the current foster parent investigation, unless we were prepared to have the Orwellian spectre of local authorities investigating all parents and interrogating them regularly as to every aspect of their social and political views.

Given, therefore, that it is an unavoidable fact that there are millions of religious parents already and they are not being deemed *ipso facto* unsuitable, it might be asked why local authorities should concern itself with the religious beliefs of prospective foster parents. Presumably, the authority would defend its position on the grounds that homosexuality has long been legal in this country and popular opinion has long moved away from discrimination on the ground of sexual orientation.

The legal position was set out by the High Court[13] as follows: there is a need to value diversity and promote equality and to

---

[12] *R (on the application of Johns and another) v Derby City Council (Equality and Human Rights Commission intervening)* [2011] All ER (D) 292 (Feb). There have been similar cases, though the blogs on which this chapter was based were written in response to the *Johns* case, and I am more interested in the point as a matter of general principle.

[13] See [2011] All ER (D) 292 (Feb). Note that the case – contrary to some published commentary – did not actually decide anything. It was dismissed

value, encourage and support children in a non-judgmental way, regardless of their sexual orientation or preference. That duty applies not only to the child and the individual placement, but to the wider context, including the main foster carer, a child's parents and the wider family, any of whom might be homosexual. In those circumstances, it is impossible to maintain that a local authority is not entitled to consider prospective foster carers' views on sexuality, least of all when it was apparent that the views held and expressed might well affect their behaviour as foster carers. Local authorities are therefore entitled to explore the extent to which prospective foster carers' beliefs might affect their behaviour and their treatment of a child being fostered by them.

That approach seems reasonably sound in logic, but there is a serious problem with the authority effectively becoming thought police. Discrimination on sexual grounds based on religion is hardly the only view considered obsolete or otherwise objectionable. Is there to be a spectrum of required political, social and religious views? Is it really the case that an otherwise upstanding citizen must be an unsuitable parent if he or she happens to have some crank views on the side?

The number of views generally considered objectionable is limited only by one's imagination. For example, how would the authority propose to deal with gay people who have openly disparaged practising Christians; adherents of any particular religion who openly disparage non-believers; adherents of any particular religion who openly discriminate against women in various respects; or representatives of any of the internecine ethnic, religious or territorial conflicts anywhere in the world who have advocated aiding or abetting combatants?

On the other hand, placing any children, still less ethnic minority children, with devout adherents of, say, the former Dutch Reformed Church would be unreasonable to say the least.

---

at a preliminary stage because the authority had not actually made any decision which might be challenged in law. Thus all discussion in the case was hypothetical or (in legal terms) *obiter*.

It does not therefore seem right to allow *carte blanche* foster placement with no investigation of prospective parents.

What, therefore, should that investigation entail? An interesting post on the case on the *UK Human Rights Blog*[14] argued that religion by definition requires a narrow minded approach to matters such as sexual orientation, blasphemy, the status of women and so on, and therefore the chances of any admitted religious adherent passing the authority's muster would be slim. They would therefore have to lie about their beliefs or not bother applying in the first place.

That may now be the law, but despite agreeing that a religion must require adherence to its own tenets and some (at least implicit) denigration of non-believers or other deviants (though not necessarily for all religions – and one further point is how to define a religion), I am not persuaded that that should be the law.

The answer, I suggest with a degree of diffidence, has to be that since people are entitled to freedom of worship in the private sphere, and freedom of expression generally, there is no getting around the fact that parents of every sort, be they natural, adoptive or foster, are bound to expose children to views which the majority would find unsavoury to say the least.

After all, a child has to be educated in the state run or state-approved school system and it is idle to assume that children will not encounter all manner of views, good, bad, arguable and indifferent in all aspects of their life. If that school system does its job properly the children will learn to question, debate and investigate views including those of their parents. And if the state is concerned about unacceptably narrow views, it should question the very concept of religious schools, which are arguably not compatible with the goal of a diverse, tolerant society, however excellent their academic results or disciplinary record.

---

[14] R. English, 'Analysis: the place of religion in foster care decisions', *UK Human Rights Blog*, 2 March 2011, http://ukhumanrightsblog. com/2011/03/02/analysis-the-place-of-religion-in-foster-care-decisions/ (Retrieved 7 February 2015).

There are many aspects of prospective foster parents that ought to be properly investigated – their financial probity and security, any criminal convictions, their reasons for wanting to become foster parents, their previous involvement with children in whatever capacity, and so forth. Their religious and political views, unless extremist, should not be towards the top of that list.[15]

---

[15] This chapter is an amalgamation of two blogs originally published on *Halsbury's Law Exchange* on 1 November 2010 and 3 March 2011 respectively.

Protecting the Vulnerable

A sad case made its way to the Court of Appeal in 2008. *City of Westminster Social & Community Services Department v KC and another*[16] concerned an attempt by a Bangladeshi couple living in Britain to have the arranged marriage of their severely handicapped son recognised in English law, notwithstanding that he lacked any capacity to marry. According to one of the judges in the Court of Appeal, Lord Justice Wall, the case highlighted 'a profound difference in culture and thinking between domestic English notions of welfare and those embraced by Islam', though I would suggest it was not so much Islamic notions but those likely to be found in any culture in countries without a welfare state.

The son was referred to throughout as IC. He was born in 1981. His intellectual impairments were severe: his mental age was less than three in most respects. He required very considerable support in all areas of his life, and he could not be left alone without risk. It was also inconceivable that he could give any form of legal consent, whether to medical treatment, marriage, sex or anything else.

The local authority had been extensively involved in supporting and protecting him since he was four years of age. In the autumn of 2006, it raised the issue of marriage with his parents. No agreement was reached and the authority therefore applied to the High Court, seeking a declaration that IC did not have the mental capacity to get married.

There was no dispute that the court had the power to prohibit the marriage of an incapacitated adult. But it emerged that the parents had already arranged a 'marriage', which they claimed had taken place in August 2006 by telephone with a bride in Bangladesh, referred to as NK. The marriage had taken the form of a 'Muslim ceremony'. The High Court declared the marriage invalid under English law and IC's parents appealed.

---

[16]   [2008] EWCA Civ 198.

Wall LJ stated:

> To the Bangladeshi mind, as admirably and clearly explained in the written evidence of the jointly instructed expert witness … the marriage of IC is perceived as a means of protecting him, and of ensuring that he is properly cared for within the family when his parents are no longer in a position to do so.
>
> To the mind of the English lawyer, by contrast, such a marriage is perceived as exploitative and indeed abusive. Under English law, a person in the position of IC is precluded from marriage for the simple reason that he lacks the capacity to marry. … Furthermore, as IC is incapable of giving his consent to any form of sexual activity, NK would commit a criminal offence in English law by attempting to have sexual intercourse ….
>
> To the mind of the English lawyer, the marriage is also exploitative of NK, although the evidence is that she entered into it with a full knowledge of IC's disability. The English lawyer inevitably poses the rhetorical question: what young woman of marriageable age, given a free choice, would ally herself for life in marriage to a man who, on the evidence, may be disturbed by her introduction into his life; for whom she will have to care as if for a child; with whom, on the evidence, she will be unable to hold a rational conversation, let alone any form of normal social intercourse; by whom she cannot have children, and indeed with whom any form of sexual contact will, under English law, as already stated, constitute a criminal offence?

He went on to declare (as did the other members of the Court, Thorpe and Hallett LJJ) that the marriage was not entitled to recognition in English law. The effect was the same as the ruling below, albeit for slightly different reasons.[17]

One can but wonder at how desperate the plight of NK and her family must have been to have entered into such an arrangement with apparent willingness. But that does not alter the fact that the right result was reached. England has a very

---

[17] The Court of Appeal held that the judge did not have jurisdiction to make a declaration that a marriage based on lack of consent was not valid under English law, since such a marriage was voidable and not void *ab intitio*. The judge should have declared that the marriage was not recognised as a valid marriage in England and Wales.

comprehensive system of caring for the handicapped. Despite the perennial complaints of underfunding, and the occasional stories of abuse or inadequacy, the system far exceeds that of most other countries – at least non-Western countries – many of which have little or no formal system at all. In such places the handicapped are usually cared for by the wider family, but that may not always be an option. Where it is not, it is entirely understandable that parents would seek to find whatever means available of ensuring that their child is cared for after they are no longer able to do so themselves. And the propensity of Westerners to dump their elderly in care homes rather than staying with the family appals many other cultures.

In Western countries, arrangements almost as one-sided as IC and NK's were not unknown before the welfare state.[18] It would be understandable for IC's parents to attempt to broker an unconventional marriage if there was no other option. But IC was entitled to – and had been receiving for most of his life – the protection of the welfare state, so there was no need for the parents to make other arrangements for his welfare. As the marriage was otherwise contrary to English law and morals, there was no justification for its recognition in England.

I do not really see that as a cultural slight, still less a religious one, and even if it was, it was not aimed at IC's particular culture or religion. The same result would have obtained if any other person of any other identity had tried to make the same arrangement for the same reasons.

---

[18] Several 'Civil War widows' in America lived to the 21st century, implausible though it may seem: during the 1920s and 30s, particularly during the Great Depression, some girls in their late teens were married off to older men for economic reasons. Some of the men, by then in their 80s, were Civil War veterans in receipt of a pension. Through the 21st century the war widow pensions were honoured (though presumably not paid in Confederate dollars).

Religion and Divorce: *The Times* Goes to the Legal Naughty Step

The Times on 1 February 2013 earned itself a spell on the 'legal naughty step', an informal censure for journalists who fail to report legal stories accurately. Its front page headline announced that a judge's decision 'opens way to divorces by Sharia'. One might expect therefore to find that the judgment in question giving rise to the headline was about Sharia law. In fact the judgment, the decision of Mr Justice Baker in the Family Court in *AI v MT*,[19] concerned a Jewish divorce under the auspices of the Beth Din, and did not mention Sharia law at all.

The parties were observant orthodox Jews. The husband was Canadian and the wife was British. They married in London in August 2006 in a Jewish religious ceremony, followed by a civil ceremony in Toronto later the same year. There were two children. Tensions arose, and the wife applied for a prohibitive steps order in England against the husband to stop him removing one of the children from her care, which is how the case first came before the courts. After negotiations, the parties agreed to consider alternative dispute resolution by means of a Beth Din hearing in New York. They signed an agreement providing for all disputes arising out of the marriage to be determined by the Beth Din.

The judge indicated that the court's jurisdiction could not be ousted in that fashion but, having regard to the parties' devout beliefs, the court would in principle be willing to endorse a process of non-binding arbitration. Further material was given to the court explaining the Beth Din's procedures. In the event the court approved a consent order giving effect to the rulings of the Beth Din.

The fact of the consent order being recognised by the High Court did not elevate the Beth Din to the status of the High Court. To the contrary, the judge stated that the following legal

[19]   [2013] EWHC 100 (Fam).

principles applied:[20] first, insofar as the court had jurisdiction to determine issues arising out of the marriage, or concerning the welfare and upbringing of the children, that jurisdiction could not be ousted by agreement. In other words, whatever the parties agreed the court would have the last word.

Secondly, save for an irrelevant exception, when considering issues concerning the upbringing of children, it was the child's welfare that was the paramount consideration. That principle runs directly counter to some religious traditions which give the wishes of the parents primacy over the welfare of the children (as for that matter English law did until fairly recently).[21]

Thirdly, the court would always give 'appropriate respect' to the cultural practice and religious beliefs of orthodox Jews, as it would to the practices of all other cultures and faiths. But that respect did not oblige the court to depart from the 'welfare of the child' principle because that was sufficiently broad and flexible to accommodate many cultural and religious practices.

Fourthly, it was always in the interests of parties to try to resolve disputes by agreement wherever possible, in the family context as much as any other.

In other words, the parties chose to resolve their differences by means of the Beth Din, but they still required the court's approval. The court happened to approve the Beth Din's ruling as reflected in the consent order, but it was the court's order, and not the Beth Din's ruling, that had force in English law. True, the result could mean that other religious rulings might in future be recognised in the same fashion, but the court's approval is not a rubber stamp. If for whatever reason (such as public policy, lack of valid consent by one or both of the parties, misrepresentation or duress) that process offended English law then the religious tribunal's decision would not be recognised and would not then attain any status in English law. And it is clear that Baker J examined the Beth Din in great detail to satisfy himself that its procedures did not offend the rights of either party under English law.

---

[20] See paras [27]–[30] of the judgment.
[21] See *Cases, Causes and Controversies*, Chapter 18.

Freedom of contract is a central concept under the common law. Arbitration – in commercial or family contexts – is but a subcategory of freedom of contract. Parties are free to agree on dispute resolution mechanisms just as they are free to agree on anything else – *within the law*. In the commercial world very sophisticated arbitration processes have developed over the years within different industries – shipping, commodity trading and so on- and London is one of the great world centres for commercial arbitration. Thus, every working day in the city tribunals constituted by grain boards or sugar boards or oil traders or whatever sit, hear evidence and decide the fate of many millions of pounds. They attempt to apply the law of the contract, which is often English law but by no means always – a Liberian shipowner might be involved in a dispute with a Manhattan broker and a London insurer and the contract might state that New York law applies. The decision of the arbitrators will be enforceable in English law if the English courts approve, and it might be challenged in the English courts under various (fairly narrow in the commercial context) provisions in the Arbitration Act 1996.

The key point is this: if the courts recognise and allow the enforcement of an arbitration conducted under (say) New York law, that involves no importation of New York law into English law. It is simply a manifestation of the common law doctrine of freedom of contract, and will have no relevance to future cases. The parties agreed they would resolve their dispute under X arbitration process pursuant to Y system of law, and unless there is a good reason (such as the examples given above regarding duress or other circumstances in which the parties cannot in fact be said to have 'agreed' despite the face of a contractual document) there is no reason why English law would not recognise it.

In the family context, the courts are more wary of straightforward enforcement of apparent agreements presented to them by consent orders, because it is rare for both parties to be sophisticated entities with independent advisers and a long history of similar transactions between them (I concede that some Hollywood stars past and present might form an exception). The courts will be even more cautious where the parties purport to resolve their differences according to a different religious or cultural tradition, because, contrary to the odd scaremongering headline, English law will not (and should not) allow what it otherwise considers persecution to be explained away for cultural or religious reasons – despite the fact that it normally tries to respect cultural and religious differences.[22] Thus, two parties could agree to a divorce under Lord of the Rings' law and if there was no countervailing reason, the courts might well agree to a consent order based on the outcome. But, for the reasons given above, that would not pave the way for fantasy books to become part of English law.

Above all, there still had to be a civil divorce. By s 44 of the Family Law Act 1986 an extra-judicial divorce (Talak or Get or any other) granted in the United Kingdom is not recognised at law; and s 46 of the same Act lays down which divorces are recognised.[23]

---

[22] A point stressed by Lady Hale in *In re J (A Child) (Custody Rights: Jurisdiction)* [2005] UKHL 40.

[23] A shorter version of this article was first published on the UK Human Rights Blog at http://ukhumanrightsblog.com/2013/02/01/court-opens-way-to-divorces-by-sharia-hold-on-a-minute-james-wilson/. I have borrowed from an excellent comment left under the article to expand the points made.

Part VI: Employment

Introduction

Employment law, residential property and family law have traditionally been among the least glamorous areas of civil law. I suspect the primary reason is that they tend to be amongst the lower paid, since they usually involve private individuals rather than large corporations. It is rather ironic, though, because for most people their jobs, family and houses are the three most important things for which they might ever consult a lawyer. Employment, family and property law, therefore ought to rank higher in the hierarchy of legal snobbery than has traditionally been the case.

Snobbery aside, employment law is one of the most controversial areas of law in theory and in practice. As a general point, most people might agree that we should not allow a return to the days of 19th-century Dickensian factories employing pre-teenage children to work all hours for a pittance. But nor would they agree that the state should own or control all of commerce: communism was the one of the great intellectual failures of the 20th century. Something in between unregulated and fully regulated employment law is therefore required.

That, I am afraid to say, is about as far towards a consensus as anyone is likely to get. Everyone is in favour of fairness until it comes to defining it. Some see a minimum wage as an obvious requirement for human decency. Others see it as either ineffective or likely to be harmful in that it will lead to a reduction in the total number of jobs available in the economy at any one time.[1]

Perhaps one other point might obtain a consensus, namely that employment law in the United Kingdom is not in a satisfactory

---

[1] See for example the editorial by Bernard Robertson in [2011] NZLJ 329. I would note that the minimum wage creates some involuntary unemployment in a simple classical economic model. In reality, however, the minimum wage only applies to a relatively small number of industries and jobs compared with the total number of jobs in the economy.

state, being far too complex. Most employment law is written by people who have no experience of being self-employed or running a small business. They do not realise that almost all employment laws (including even the idea of weekends and public holidays) have no relevance to the self-employed, while small businesses can rarely spare the resources to pour over the minutiae of reams of red tape pertaining to employment laws or other regulatory requirements.

All that said, lawyers may ultimately overstate their own importance in the employment sphere (as elsewhere). It seems to me that there is only one certain form of protection for workers, with regard to wages or working conditions, and that is a competitive market for their services. Unfortunately, in an increasingly globalised environment, with free movement of workers, such a market looks increasingly unlikely, especially for low-skilled jobs.

Yet another contentious area of employment law concerns the application of human rights to employment relationships. The following chapters consider the appropriate circumstances, if any, in which an employee's political or religious beliefs should be relevant to their job. Is there room for freedom of speech and freedom of religion in the workplace? Whose freedom should it be – the freedom of an employer to hire only those who share the same beliefs, or the right of a prospective employee not to be discriminated against because of his or hers? As I have already said, the chances of a consensus emerging appear slim.

Employment and Religion

The post-war development of human rights and equality as legal concepts has had many manifestations. One concerns the right to religious beliefs. On its face, this right in the employment context seems uncontroversial. Someone should not be fired or otherwise discriminated simply because of their personal religious beliefs, at least on the assumption that those beliefs do not interfere with their ability to do their job. But, as the case of *Nicholson v Grainger plc*[2] demonstrates, it is one thing to have an uncontroversial idea, but quite another to transpose it into uncontroversial regulation.

The case concerned the Employment Equality (Religion or Belief) Regulations 2003 (EER 2003). Paragraph 2(1) provided:

> (1) In these Regulations – i. 'religion' means any religion, ii. 'belief' means any religious or philosophical belief, iii. a reference to religion includes a reference to lack of religion, and iv. a reference to belief includes a reference to lack of belief.

It is easy imagine the thought process which led to para 2(1). The starting point would have been the notion referred to above, namely not discriminating against a particular religion (human history being riddled with odious examples of religious minorities being persecuted). Secularists objected to religion receiving apparently preferential treatment, hence the definition of belief was extended to include 'absence of belief', however inaccurately that may define atheism.

It is, however, illogical to single out religious beliefs (and the positive absence thereof) for special protection, even if one could define religion satisfactorily to begin with. In the United States in the 1960s, if one could prove to the authorities' satisfaction that one was a practising Quaker, then, without more, one might gain exemption from the Vietnam War draft. Yet someone who had, say, written a brilliant Harvard PhD on pacifism, would not have had the same exemption. It is not clear

---

[2]   [2009] All ER (D) 59 (Nov).

why the hypothetical Harvard scholar would have had a weaker case for exemption than a Quaker.[3]

Presumably in response to such concerns the definition for the purposes of the British regulation was extended to include philosophical beliefs, presumably to cover secular philosophies as pacifism, and it was under this aspect of the definition that Nicholson alleged that his climate change principles fell. He contended that he believed that 'we must urgently cut carbon emissions to avoid catastrophic climate change.'

One objection is that such a contention does not really amount to a philosophy, but rather a view on a disputed area of science. In fact, proponents of the anthropological global warming theory (AGW) are usually anxious that the theory is not classified as philosophy or religion, or its scientific credibility might be undermined. Either the greenhouse gas emissions from industrial or other human activities are having a significant detrimental effect on the atmosphere or they are not. Such is to be proved or disproved like any other scientific theory.

The judge, Burton J, was not troubled by that point. He said:

> In my judgment, if a person can establish that he holds a philosophical belief which is based on science, as opposed, for example, to religion, then there is no reason to disqualify it from protection by the Regulations. The Employment Judge drew attention to the existence of empiricist philosophers, no doubt such as Hume and Locke. The best example, as it seems to me, which was canvassed during the course of the hearing, is by reference to the clash of two such philosophies, exemplified in the play *Inherit the Wind*, i.e. one not simply between those who supported Creationism and those who did not, but between those who positively supported, and wished to teach, only Creationism and those who positively supported, and wished to teach, only Darwinism. Darwinism must plainly be capable of being a philosophical belief, albeit that it may be based entirely on scientific conclusions (not all of which may be uncontroversial).

---

[3]   See *Cases, Causes and Controversies*, Chapter 17.

I do not see how it can be argued that Darwinism is a philosophical belief – either it is true we are evolved from other forms of life or it is not. It may not be possible to prove it to every scientist's satisfaction, but that does not move the theory into the realms of philosophy, it simply leaves it as an unproven scientific theory, as for example the tectonic plate theory once was. Nevertheless, for the purposes of the regulations, discriminating against someone because of their acceptance of the theory of evolution is at least as objectionable as discriminating against them because of their philosophical beliefs, so for that reason it is arguable that we should live with Darwinism and climate change being lumped in with 'philosophy' however objectionable that might be to a scientist – unless the definition is altered yet again to include 'scientific belief' as well.

That line of thinking seems to be heading therefore to a regulation that covers more or less any sort of belief whatsoever. During the course of the judgment Burton J also stated that 'philosophical belief' could include political belief. This seems unobjectionable: Marxism, or the theories of John Rawls, or Robert Nozick (or innumerable others), can properly be described as philosophy.

At various points Burton J caught himself short on two grounds: first, that some religions or belief systems are objectionable, such as discriminating against women, other ethnicities and so on; and secondly, some might be seen as trivial (he specifically mentioned the Jedi religion to which many in a 21st-century British census claimed to subscribe). Having reviewed various authorities he came up with the following mesh to sift out offending belief systems: (i) the belief had to be genuinely held; (ii) it had to be a belief and not an opinion or viewpoint based on the present state of information available; (iii) it had to be a belief as to a weighty and substantial aspect of human life and behaviour; (iv) it had to attain a certain level of cogency, seriousness, cohesion and importance; and (v) it had to be worthy of respect in a democratic society, not be incompatible with human dignity and not conflict with the fundamental rights of others.

In other words it has to be a belief system of which the state approves. We can I suppose simply be grateful that the present state of the United Kingdom is fairly tolerant by historical standards in that regard.[4]

But it is still a fundamental flawed approach. It should not be necessary to define belief, or scientific belief, or philosophical belief, or any other such byzantine question. People should not be fired from their jobs due to their religious beliefs. They should instead only be fired for things that are relevant to the job. Since religion is not, and insofar as it is not, then people should not be fired because of it. So all the courts should need to do is look at whether there was any compelling reason for the person to get fired, such as that they were not doing the job.

There remains some further confusion about the consequences of belief protection. It is quite proper that someone should not be fired because they hold certain beliefs, but at the same time there is a problem if they start to contend that their beliefs impose positive requirements on their employer. For example, they might argue that they need prayer facilities at the employer's expense, time out for prayer during the day and religious festivals (without any obligation to make up the time later), and to be excused from doing certain tasks on the ground that their religion precludes it, for example selling meat if they are a vegetarian.

The answer is that the obligation in a free society is that one is required to respect a person's right to their beliefs, but not to respect for the beliefs themselves. It would be perfectly acceptable for an employee to hold her religious beliefs, but not to impose any cost on her employer or her fellow employees to accommodate them. Otherwise it is compelling them at least partly to accept those beliefs, which might or might not be

---

[4]   Since the decision the Supreme Court in the case of *R (on the application of Hodkin) v Registrar-General of Births, Deaths and Marriages* [2013] UKSC 77 chose a much more expansive definition of religion. See *Cases that Changed Our Lives*, vol II, p 157.

contrary to their own. The employee should not therefore take on the job in the first place, or should negotiate the terms before she starts. Regrettably, no such straightforward solution seems to be preferred by the courts nowadays.

On the Buses: Employment and Politics

The British National Party (BNP) considers the European Convention on Human Rights to be a means by which Britain may be exploited by 'the world's scroungers'. Its manifesto promises to scrap the Convention the moment it gains power. It was therefore with a tinge of irony in late 2012 that one of the BNP's members actually managed to win a case in Strasbourg based on the rights protected by the Convention.[5] The case is a good example of the rule of law in action, in two senses. First, the law applies equally to everyone, including members of unpopular political parties. Secondly, if exceptions to general rules are generated out of sympathy to particular classes of people, injustice will swiftly follow as other equally worthy classes are identified as not qualifying for the same exception.

The claimant, Redfearn, was a bus driver. He was employed by a private company, Serco Ltd (Serco), which in turn supplied services to a local authority. There were no complaints about the standard of his work and in fact his supervisor, who was of Asian origin, had nominated him for the award of 'first class employee'.

Redfearn's political affiliation became known to the public when he was elected as a city councillor. A number of complaints were received from unions and employees, following which he was dismissed by Serco. The grounds given for dismissal were that he would present a risk to the 'health and safety' of his co-workers and passengers, and that he would jeopardise the reputation of his employer. Those grounds were based on the simple fact of his membership of the BNP, rather than anything he had actually done during the course of his employment.

Redfearn challenged his dismissal without success in the domestic courts before winning in Europe. It needs to be emphasised, however, that his victory in Strasbourg was only on a preliminary point. Redfearn wished to argue that he had been unfairly dismissed on account of his political beliefs or

---

[5]   *Redfearn v United Kingdom* (App. No. 47335/06) [2012] ECHR 1878.

affiliations. He was precluded from doing so by the requirement of domestic law that required a year's service before such complaints could be made (the 'one-year rule'). The one-year rule did not, however, apply to grounds of pregnancy, race, sex or religion. The majority of the Strasbourg court found that the one-year rule therefore needed to be reconsidered and expanded to include political opinion or affiliation, or a free-standing cause of action to the same effect.

Here is a classic example of why exceptions from a general rule – in other words, breaches of the rule of law – are a minefield. The one-year rule was thought by Parliament to be necessary to encourage employers to take on more staff, since it gave them a cushion to let the staff go if they were not up to scratch or if economic circumstances changed. Then it was thought that some forms of ill treatment, such as discrimination, were so serious that some exceptions should be made to the general rule. Then, almost inevitably, more exceptions were found necessary, after expensive litigation, leaving the question of whether still more might be found in the future or whether deserving claimants will be left without a remedy.

Employers would not be happy with the resultant confusion and uncertainty, and some no doubt would be more cautious about hiring new staff as a result – the very opposite of what Parliament was trying to achieve with the one-year rule in the first place.[6]

Let us return therefore to the substantive dispute. Without belittling the skill and responsibility involved, if Redfearn's job was simply to drive a bus it is hard to see how his political affiliations (or, equally, had they been in issue, his religious or philosophical beliefs) would have been relevant. They might have been if he had chosen to display them by symbols, or logos, or if he had been covered in aggressive or offensive tattoos (both of which would then raise an issue of freedom of expression); or

---

[6] Another side issue concerns the application of the Convention to a private employment contract, and whether Serco was in fact equivalent to an arm of the state because it was supplying services for the local authority. I leave that aside for now.

if he had decided to treat his passengers differently according to their race or gender or appearance.

One of the key principles behind anti-discrimination laws – ironically the very type the BNP generally opposes – is that people should not be subject to different treatment in employment for irrelevant reasons. Race, gender, political opinions and membership of a lawful political organisation are irrelevant to many jobs and certainly, one would have thought, driving a bus.

If the driver's performance was satisfactory, then membership of a legal organisation would not be grounds for dismissal but instead an exercise of the basic human right of freedom of association, even if it involved associating with a group that would, if given the chance, remove a few basic human rights.

Then there is the question, which was in fact raised in Redfearn's case, whether he could have been moved to a non-customer facing role. If so, suppose Redfearn changed his mind and disowned the BNP: would he then be able to demand reinstatement to his previous role or at least reconsideration of his suitability elsewhere? Would there be a test of his sincerity? If so, would that be amenable to review by the employment tribunal?

The BNP is a party that has obtained minimal success at the ballot box, and most commentators dismiss it as an intolerant irrelevance. But here we have the classic liberal dilemma of 'tolerating intolerance'. A more tolerant society than the one the BNP would like to create has to tolerate dissent, and even highly objectionable opinions, in the name of free speech, free association and freedom of religion.[7]

One only has to look at how political undesirables are treated in many other countries to realise that toleration of minority views, even what the majority finds extremely objectionable

---

[7]   When I first published a version of this article online, I received a comment from an anonymous BNP member explaining that what I had written was 'a load of rubbish'. It also explained what the author thought of the religion of Islam. Neither point went very far towards addressing the arguments put forward in the article. Readers are invited to read the BNP's website (if one remains extant) and other literature and form their own views.

minority views, is a fundamental requirement for democracy and freedom. Then there is the employment law perspective, outlined above in the chapter on *Nicholson v Grainger plc*: people should only be promoted, demoted or fired for reasons connected with and relevant to their employment.

As I have argued in respect of various other cases,[8] homosexuals should not be discriminated against in the provision of services offered to the public, even if it offends the sincerely held religious beliefs of others. Nor should people be denied the ability to wear religious dress in public. Nor should people be sent to jail for writing offensive material on the internet. And people should not be dismissed from their jobs for holding political views (or any other reason) unless those views preclude them from doing their jobs properly – in which case it is their performance, not their views, which should be impugned.

---

[8]   See *Cases that Changed Our Lives*, vol II, p 151.

Employment and Facebook

The previous chapter argued that someone's political views ought not to be a ground for dismissal or discipline unless they were somehow relevant to the job. The case of *Smith v Trafford Housing Trust*[9] provides another, even clearer, example of the same principle.

The claimant, Smith, was employed as a housing manager by the defendant, a private housing trust. In February 2011 he placed a link on his Facebook page to a BBC news article about gay marriages in church, and added the comment 'an equality too far'. On the same day one of his Facebook friends responded with the comment 'Does this mean you don't approve?' Smith replied:

> No not really, I don't understand why people who have no faith and don't believe in Christ would want to get hitched in church the bible is quite specific that marriage is for men and women if the state wants to offer civil marriage to same sex then that is up to the state; but the state shouldn't impose it's (sic) rules on places of faith and conscience.

For making those comments Smith was suspended from work on full pay and subjected to disciplinary proceedings, leading to a hearing in March 2011 at which he was told he was guilty of gross misconduct justifying his dismissal. Because of his good service record, he was instead demoted to a non-managerial position, with a consequential 40% pay reduction, phased over 12 months. His subsequent internal appeal was effectively dismissed, though with an extension of the phasing-in of the salary reduction from one to two years. He issued proceedings in the High Court, contending that the defendant had breached his contract by the demotion and pay reduction.

Smith argued that he had not been guilty of gross misconduct, or any misconduct at all, in posting the Facebook comments. The defendant countered that he had committed breaches of its code of conduct for employees and acted contrary to its equal opportunities policy.

---

[9]   [2012] EWHC 3221 (Ch).

The judge held that a reasonable reader of Smith's Facebook wall page could not rationally conclude that the two postings about gay marriage in church had been made in any relevant sense on the defendant's behalf. The brief mention on his Facebook page of the identity of his employer was in no way inconsistent with the general impression to be gained from his Facebook wall – namely, that it was a medium for personal or social, rather than work related, information and views.

That was not to say that Facebook could never be used as a medium for work related communications, but clearly Smith had not been using it in that fashion. Any reader would be left in no doubt that he regarded his employment merely as a fact – and not a particularly interesting fact – about himself. Nor were his postings about gay marriage in church themselves work related.

It seems to me that the judge's findings constituted blunt common sense. Apart from anything else, putting the case at its highest in the defendant's favour – that is to say, assuming that the comments could in some way be linked to Smith's employment – it is still hard to see how the defendant could have been justified in demoting him. As the judge said, Smith's posts were not judgemental, disrespectful or liable to cause upset or offence. They were widely held views frequently to be heard on radio and television, or read in the newspapers. His comment was made in response to an enquiry as to his views, and it was given in moderate language unlikely to offend anyone, even strong supporters of gay marriage.

Smith's claim therefore succeeded. Unfortunately, the correct measure of damages was held to be the difference between Smith's contractual salary and the amount actually paid to him during the 12 weeks following his assumption of his new, but reduced, role. That was a very modest sum and rendered his victory somewhat pyrrhic. The judge expressed 'real disquiet' about that fact – Smith, he reiterated, had been taken to task for doing nothing wrong, suspended and subjected to a disciplinary procedure which had wrongly found him guilty of gross misconduct, and then demoted to a non-managerial post with an eventual 40% reduction in salary. The breach of contract which the defendant thereby committed was serious and repudiatory (meaning that Smith would have been entitled to treat his employment at an end). The defendant was therefore very lucky to get off so lightly in financial terms.

I suspect that the defendant was acting out of the laudable motive to be seen to be an equal opportunities employer, and not to be seen to endorse any views that were discriminatory towards any potential customers. Those are understandable aims, but they do not justify the sort of action that was taken against Smith. Employers do not need to be thought police. If Smith held some views which he only ever expressed in his personal capacity, that was his business – unless perhaps they called into question his sanity, incited violence or were directed at potential customers.

One feels that a disturbing climate is generated by these sorts of cases, in which all employees are expected to be on message politically – something ironically inimical to the notion of a diverse, tolerant society, which has to tolerate dissent and a wide range of views, even those counter to the *zeitgeist*, as argued in respect of Redfearn in the previous chapter.

The overarching principle for cases such as Smith's is, once again, that employees should only be hired or fired, promoted or demoted, according to actions relevant to their job. If they express views in private that have no bearing on their performance at work and in no way related to their employer, it is hard to see why they should be sanctioned by the employer, even if the views are ones which the employer does not share.

Harassment and His Holiness

It is as well that one Mr Heafield did not get a job in the timber yards where I worked over a couple of summers as a student. For the majority of the staff and customers the use of the 'f word' was not so much bad language as a way of life. It was rare that they would manage a sentence without it, unless a female was present, in which case its use would be watered down to every other sentence. I was always amused by the fact that sometimes they could use it the same sentence as a noun, adjective and verb, and yet still convey their meaning perfectly.

Heafield worked as a casual sub-editor in the slightly more rarefied environment of *The Times* newspaper in London. He was there during the time of the Pope's visit to the United Kingdom in 2010. On the evening of 12 March, the news desk was preparing a story about allegations that the Pope had protected a paedophile priest. One of the editors, a Mr Wilson (no relation), shouted across to the senior production executives *'Can anyone tell what's happening to the fucking Pope?'* When there was no response he repeated the question more loudly.

Heafield, a Roman Catholic, took offence at Wilson's inquiry. He raised a complaint with management, which in his view was not properly progressed, and he then brought a claim in the employment tribunal for harassment and victimisation on the ground of his religious belief.

The definition of harassment at the time was contained in reg 5 of the Employment Equality (Religion or Belief) Regulations 2003 (since replaced by the Equality Act 2010). Regulation 5 provided:

(1) For the purposes of these Regulations, a person ('A') subjects another person ('B') to harassment where, on grounds of religion or belief, A engages in unwanted conduct which has the purpose or effect of –

(a) violating B's dignity; or

(b) creating an intimidating, hostile, degrading, humiliating or offensive environment for B.

(2) Conduct shall be regarded as having the effect specified in paragraph (1)(a) or (b) only if, having regard to all the circumstances, including in particular the perception of B, it should reasonably be considered as having that effect.

The tribunal adopted the same approach as had been followed under the Race Relations Act 1976 by the Employment Appeal Tribunal in *Richmond Pharmaceuticals v Dhaliwal*:[10]

As a matter of formal analysis it is not difficult to break down the necessary elements of liability under section 3A. They can be expressed as three-fold:

(1) The unwanted conduct: Did the Respondent engage in unwanted conduct;

(2) The purpose or effect of that conduct: Did the conduct in question either

(a) have the purpose or,

(b) have the effect

of either (i) violating the claimant's dignity or (ii) creating an adverse environment for her. ...

(3) The grounds for the conduct. Was that conduct on the grounds of the Claimant's race (or ethnic or national origins)?

The tribunal went on to hold that Wilson's bad language was merely an expression of bad temper, which might have amounted to 'unwanted conduct', but was not intended to express hostility to the Pope or Roman Catholicism. Element (1) of the test in *Richmond Pharmaceuticals* had therefore been established but not elements (2) or (3). Wilson had not known that Heafield was Catholic and, more to the point, there had been no anti-Catholic purpose in what he said. His use of the f-word was simply a manifestation of his stress at the time.

---

[10]   [2009] ICR 724.

By a fairly tortuous route, the details of which can be ignored for the present, the matter ended up before the Employment Appeal Tribunal.[11]

The Appeal Tribunal held that the employment tribunal had been plainly right in finding that, to the extent that Heafield felt his dignity to be violated or that an adverse environment had been created, that was not a reasonable reaction. It stated:

> What Mr Wilson said was not only not ill-intentioned or anti-Catholic or directed at the Pope or at Catholics: it was evidently not any of those things. No doubt in a perfect world he should not have used an expletive in the context of a sentence about the Pope, because it might be taken as disrespectful by a pious Catholic of tender sensibilities, but people are not perfect and sometimes use bad language thoughtlessly: a reasonable person would have understood that and made allowance for it.

Element (2) had therefore not been satisfied and accordingly the appeal would fail without needing to consider element (3).

Far too often in different contexts courts have had to consider claims for compensation on the ground that someone has been 'offended' without any more tangible loss or damage than that. One can no doubt imagine situations in which such offence or hostility is generated that it amounts to harassment or an impossible working environment, but Heafield's case as presented to the employment tribunal came nowhere near.

Legend has it that during the infamous 'Bodyline' cricket series between Australia and England in the early 1930s the England captain, Douglas Jardine, went to the Australian dressing room after a day's play to complain that he had been called a 'bastard' by one of the Australian team. He demanded an apology. The Australian captain turned to his team and shouted inquiringly 'Alright, which one of you bastards called this bastard a bastard?'

History has not been enormously kind to Jardine, who is generally remembered as a pompous sort whose actions on and off the pitch were rarely to be admired. Heafield might take note.

---

[11]   See *Heafield v Times Newspaper Ltd (Religion or Belief Discrimination)* [2013] UKEAT 1305_12_1701.

Part VII: Civil Law

Introduction

Civil law is perhaps most easily defined by what it is not: it is not criminal law. But it is everything else, or at least all other forms of domestic law. Hence any time one private individual or other legal personality sues another, the case falls under the broad heading 'civil law'.

We begin with two great negligence cases, the first of which is arguably the most famous civil case in English history (despite being a Scottish case): *Donoghue v Stevenson*. The basic principle of the case – that someone can be held liable to someone else, even if they did not voluntarily conclude an agreement beforehand – is not only the founding principle of modern consumer law, but much more of the common law besides. One manifestation is the sort of negligence cases which occasionally get a bad press for comprising 'ambulance chasing' lawyers. The second case considered here, *Tomlinson v Congleton Borough Council & Ors*, has been seen as an attempt by the courts to put a brake on that sort of claim.

We then have a series of spicy, salacious and occasionally ridiculous libel claims. Julie Burchill's case can be described without hyperbole as one of the most absurd libel actions in English history. The judgment of the majority of the Court of Appeal is regrettably an example of highly intelligent people faced with an unreasonable question and unfortunately coming up with an unreasonable answer. The dissenting judgment of Lord Justice Millett, on the other hand, gives a pithy and reasonable response to the same question.

In the middle of those cases is something entirely different: the tale of Col. A. D. Wintle, one of the great English eccentrics. I have included his case in the civil law section because he managed the extraordinary feat of becoming the first unrepresented litigant to win a case before the highest court of the land. But, as will be seen, that was about the least of Wintle's life achievements. I wonder if there is anyone like him alive today?

We finish the civil law section with some cases about authorship of artistic or otherwise original work. Here there are a number of interesting questions, not the least of which is, how does the law decide who the true composer of a piece might be? In one of the cases discussed,[1] the judge explained the law in these terms:

42. By virtue of Schedule 1 paragraph 10 of the Copyright Designs and Patents Act 1988, authorship of copyright in an existing work is governed by the relevant provisions of the Copyright Act 1956. Section 11(3) of that Act provides that:

'In this Act 'work of joint authorship' means a work produced by the collaboration of two or more authors in which the contribution of each author is not separate from the contribution of the other author or authors.'

43. There are therefore three requirements which must be met before a work can be regarded as a work of joint authorship:

i) there must be collaboration in the creation of the work;

ii) there must be a contribution from each joint author;

iii) the contribution must not be 'separate'.

44. The collaboration required is 'joint labouring in the furtherance of a common design' see *Levy v Rutley* (1871) LR 6 CP 523. Subsequent independent alteration of a finished work will not give rise to work of joint authorship.

45. Clearly, trivial contributions will not qualify the contributor as a joint author. Moreover the contribution made must be of 'the right kind of skill and labour': all collaborators must answer to the description 'author'. Mere suggestions or ideas may not be enough. It has been said that the contribution of the co-author to the creation of the musical work must be 'significant and original': see e.g. *Hadley v Kemp* [1999] EMLR 589 at 643. Ultimately the question has been said to be one of fact and degree.

---

[1] *Beckingham v Hodgens and others* [2002] All ER (D) 24 (Jul).

Needless to say, questions of 'fact and degree' usually leave room for argument, though I have yet to think of a better alternative.

Snails and Ginger Beer

'Not for me to expound the implications of *Donoghue v Stevenson*. To be quite candid, I detest that snail.'

Lord Justice MacKinnon[2]

One of the defining features of the common law is that it has developed not from complex rules delivered from on high, but rather from the courts recognising and enforcing private bargains voluntarily concluded by ordinary citizens. There can be no better example than *Donoghue v Stevenson*, perhaps the most recognisable civil case of all – certainly in respect of its imagery of a snail emerging from a ginger beer bottle. Just over eighty years after the House of Lords ruled on the case, it still features among the top ten most viewed cases on most legal databases.

The story begins on 26 August 1928, when Mrs Donoghue entered the Wellmeadow Café in Paisley with a friend. The friend bought a drink for herself and a 'ginger beer ice cream float' for Donoghue. The café's owner, Francis Minghella, poured some of the ginger beer over the ice cream to create the 'float'. Donoghue drank some and her friend then poured the rest of the bottle into a glass, whereupon the partially decomposed snail of legend emerged.

Donoghue claimed to have suffered shock and severe gastroenteritis as a result. She sued the manufacturer of the ginger beer, which turned out to be a family business run by one David Stevenson, located no more than a mile from the Wellmeadow Café.

All hinged on the point that the friend, not Donoghue herself, had paid for the drink. Had it been otherwise, Donoghue could simply have sued Minghella in contract (the friend could not because it was Donoghue who had suffered the harm) and

---

[2] Quoted in Matthew Chapman, *The Snail and the Ginger Beer* (Wildy, Simmonds & Hill, 2010), p 16.

the modern law of negligence would have had to have been invented at the behest of someone else.

Interestingly, all of those famous facts might be no more than mere speculation. They were never actually tested in court since the point of law which found its way into the law reports was heard as a preliminary issue, and the dispute was later settled before trial.

The preliminary issue was whether Donoghue could establish that Stevenson had owed her any duty of care. The Scottish appeal court said she could not, reasoning on earlier authority that since the ginger beer was not considered a dangerous product as such, and there had been no fraudulent misrepresentation by the manufacturer, Donoghue had no cause of action. All seemed lost.

But no one had counted on the tenacity of Donoghue's solicitor, the appropriately-named Walter Leecham. He seems to have had a thing for dodgy ginger beer cases, having earlier brought an action involving the even more alarming corpse of a mouse (at this point even the most ardent Luddite of readers might start to be grateful for modern manufacturing processes, or at least transparent bottles). He took Donoghue's case *pro bono*, and the courts declared Donoghue a 'pauper' and therefore not liable for the defendant's legal costs – hence she was able to appeal to the House of Lords.

No lawyer will need reminding of what happened: the majority ruled in Donoghue's favour, with Lord Atkin uttering the immortal words (drawing on the Biblical parable of the *Good Samaritan*):

> You must take reasonable care to avoid acts or omissions which you can reasonably foresee would be likely to injure your neighbour. Who then, in law is my neighbour? The answer seems to be persons who are so closely and directly affected in my act that I ought reasonably to have them in contemplation as being so affected when I am directing my mind to the acts or omissions which are called into question.

> Since it was eminently reasonable that Stevenson should have had in mind the person who would ultimately drink his ginger

beer, and should therefore have taken more care about what fell into it, Donoghue succeeded.

And so the modern law of negligence began. In the eighty years since, the concept has been developed further by such great cases as *Hedley, Byrne & Co Ltd v Heller & Partners Ltd* and *Caparo v Dickman*. Anyone in Donoghue's unfortunate position can now rely on the (perhaps excessive) plethora of regulations that comprise present-day consumer protection, almost all of which owe something in terms of their theoretical underpinnings to *Donoghue v Stevenson*.

Except it wasn't quite such a seamless process. A number of years elapsed between the decision of the House of Lords and the general realisation of how widely Lord Atkin's neighbour principle could be applied. Certainly the editor of the official law reports at the time seems to have missed the significance, the headnote[3] effectively confining the *ratio* to manufacturers of food or similar, with no indication of the myriad of circumstances to which it was subsequently applied.

Others considered that Lord Atkin's judgment did not reflect the opinion of the majority anyway, because the other two judges did not use the same terminology and their speeches seemed less far-reaching.[4]

Nevertheless, Lord Atkin's speech became firmly established as the first port of call for anyone trying to decide whether person A should have had person B in mind before performing whatever action or omission led to B's harm. It also remains a popular destination for law book designers wondering what picture to put on the cover ...[5]

---

[3] [1932] AC 562.
[4] The full history of the case is set out by Matthew Chapman in *The Snail and the Ginger Beer*, supra.
[5] Published in the *New Law Journal*, vol 163, 11 October 2013, p 22.

Look Before You Leap

For many years the British media has enjoyed something of a jaundiced laugh at the expense of the supposed American 'compensation culture': stories about people suing fast-food chains because their coffee was too hot, or car manufacturers because they did not realise that 'cruise control' did not mean the car would drive itself, and so on. In more recent times, there has been some evidence of Britain going down the same road. After the rules about funding personal injury claims were changed to allow no-win no-fee arrangements, advertisements started appearing in many places for ambulance-chasing lawyers asking enthusiastically whether viewers or readers had had an accident in the past few years and whether they felt like suing over it. It was therefore to the relief of many when, in 2003, a judgment of the House of Lords went some way towards pouring the compensation-culture genie back into its bottle.

In May 1995, 18-year-old John Tomlinson went to Brereton Heath Country Park, between Holmes Chapel and Congleton. The park had been created about 15 years earlier by Congleton Borough Council on the site of a derelict quarry. The quarry itself had been turned into a lake. Tomlinson ran into the water and dived into the lake, as he had done many times before. On the day in question, something went disastrously wrong, as Tomlinson hit his head on the lake bottom and broke his fifth vertebra. He was left a tetraplegic.

Understandably devastated, Tomlinson decided to sue the local authority,[6] alleging that it had created a hazard in the form of the lake and that, under the Occupiers' Liability Acts 1957 and 1984, it owed a duty to members of the public such as himself to warn of the danger. He claimed that the authority was in breach of that duty.

His claim faced some formidable obstacles. The council had placed warning signs stating that not just diving but swimming was prohibited. Tomlinson argued that the warning signs were

---

[6] There was some preliminary legal skirmishing over which local authority was the appropriate defendant, but I will leave that aside.

inadequate, but admitted that he had known of them. That was enough to defeat his claim under the 1957 Act, but not under the different scope of the 1984 Act.

The trial judge held that the danger and risk of injury from diving in the lake where it was shallow were obvious, and there was no breach by the authority of any duty. Tomlinson appealed.

Somewhat surprisingly, the Court of Appeal, by a majority, allowed Tomlinson's appeal.[7] Lord Justices Ward and Sedley held that there was a duty on the authority, on the particular facts of the case. Prior to the accident, the authority had identified the risk of people swimming, and considered that various landscaping and planting measures should be taken to discourage it. Those measures had not in fact been carried out, despite costing only a modest amount. The failure to take the measures meant that the authority could properly be held liable.

Perhaps aware of the controversial nature of their decision, Ward and Sedley LJJ were keen to stress that the case turned on its particular facts, and would not necessarily require the same result if someone else was injured swimming in a different lake if the circumstances were not otherwise identical. Nevertheless, the authority appealed to the House of Lords.

The House of Lords was clearly unimpressed with the case.[8] In blunt yet colourful language, Lord Hoffmann said:

> If people want to climb mountains, go hang gliding or swim or dive in ponds or lakes, that is their affair. Of course the landowner may for his own reasons wish to prohibit such activities. He may be think that they are a danger or inconvenience to himself or others. Or he may take a paternalist view and prefer people not to undertake risky activities on his land. He is entitled to impose such conditions, as the Council did by prohibiting swimming. But the law does not require him to do so.

Lord Hobhouse said:

> [I]t is not, and should never be, the policy of the law to require the protection of the foolhardy or reckless few to deprive, or

---

[7]   *Tomlinson v Congleton Borough Council & Ors* [2001] EWCA Civ 911. Longmore LJ dissented.

[8]   *Tomlinson v Congleton Borough Council & Ors* [2003] UKHL 47.

interfere with, the enjoyment by the remainder of society of the liberties and amenities to which they are rightly entitled. Does the law require that all trees be cut down because some youths may climb them and fall? Does the law require the coast line and other beauty spots to be lined with warning notices? Does the law require that attractive water side picnic spots be destroyed because of a few foolhardy individuals who choose to ignore warning notices and indulge in activities dangerous only to themselves? The answer to all these questions is, of course, no. But this is the road down which your Lordships, like other courts before, have been invited to travel and which the councils in the present case found so inviting. In truth, the arguments for the claimant have involved an attack upon the liberties of the citizen which should not be countenanced. They attack the liberty of the individual to engage in dangerous, but otherwise harmless, pastimes at his own risk and the liberty of citizens as a whole fully to enjoy the variety and quality of the landscape of this country. The pursuit of an unrestrained culture of blame and compensation has many evil consequences and one is certainly the interference with the liberty of the citizen.

It seems to me that the decision of the House of Lords constituted elementary common sense and that it was correctly hailed as a brake on the ever-creeping compensation culture. Since Tomlinson had known that swimming was not permitted, and as an intelligent adult should have known that diving was dangerous in the area, to suggest there was some form of causation involved in his injury, other than his own bad judgement, was just plain wrong. I agree in particular with the point that there is nothing inherently dangerous about the side of a mountain; it only becomes dangerous if someone tries to climb it. And if they do, assuming they are a competent adult, they should do so at their own risk.

The Last Englishman Wins a First in Court

For most barristers, winning a case in the highest court of the land would count as something of a career highlight. For anyone else, it would be something quite extraordinary. For Col. Alfred Wintle MC, however, becoming the first ever litigant in person to win a case before the House of Lords was arguably not even his most interesting legal experience, never mind life experience. Wintle was an adventurer whose life story might have stretched the imagination of W. E. Johns or George MacDonald Fraser, and his various brushes with authority were often as comical as they were bizarre.

Wintle's autobiography was appropriately entitled *The Last Englishman*, although as the son of a diplomat he was born in Russia and grew up primarily on the Continent. He spoke French and German fluently, although he despised the locals, once giving thanks for being born an Englishman, as opposed to 'a chimpanzee, or a flea, a Frenchman or a German'. A further clue to his character is that he only unfurled his umbrella once in his lifetime – to insert a note saying 'This umbrella was stolen from Col A.D. Wintle'. 'No true gentleman would ever unfurl one' he later explained.

During the Great War, on Wintle's first night at the Western Front, his sergeant was killed by artillery fire, covering Wintle with his remains. Wintle nevertheless remained as resolute as if on parade, later attributing his stoicism to being 'an Englishman of action'.

Later in the war he claimed to have captured a village single-handedly. His luck finally ran out at Ypres, where he injured a hand, lost a kneecap and lost his left eye, while his right eye was damaged so badly that he was forced to wear a monocle. Those injuries amounted to a 'Blighty' and Wintle was duly removed to a hospital in England. Far from being relieved, he was apoplectic at the thought of missing the rest of the war, and so escaped from the hospital when the staff's backs were turned (though not before attempting to attend a nurses-only ball in disguise; apparently his monocle gave him away).[9] He eventually made it back to the front, where he earned the MC just before the war ended.

Wintle found himself most inconvenienced by the Armistice. He wrote in his diary that he was declaring 'private war on Germany', and helped pass the time by writing fiction – under a *nom de plume*, since he thought it would not do for a cavalry officer to be seen to be literate.

In the Second World War, after Pétain threw in the French towel, Wintle demanded an aircraft at gunpoint from 'some inconsiderable civil servant' (actually an RAF Air Commodore), intending to fly to France to rally their beleaguered forces. He was arrested and sent to the Tower of London. On the way his hapless guard lost the arrest warrant; Wintle, a stickler for military standards, demanded that it be replaced. When no senior officer was available, he signed the new warrant himself.

He was treated in the Tower like royalty, with comfortable surroundings and generous visiting rights. He was assigned a batman, but continued to polish his own kit as he thought an ordinary solider would not be able to maintain a cavalry officer's equipment to the appropriate standard. At his court-martial, he faced three charges (i) faking injuries in order to avoid active duty, (ii) assaulting an officer and (iii) conduct contrary to (and to the prejudice of) good order and military discipline.

Wintle easily disproved the first charge by adducing medical evidence. He enthusiastically admitted the other two, producing a list of other people whom he thought ought to be shot for being unpatriotic. No doubt partly due to governmental embarrassment about his list, the third charge was dropped and only a formal reprimand was issued for the second. It may

---

[9]   Between the wars, Wintle again spent some time in hospital, this time with a broken leg after a riding accident. Whilst there he was told that one of the other patients was a trooper in the Dragoon Guards and was at death's door. Wintle climbed out of bed and tore a strip off the soldier in question, telling him he was not to die without permission, and that he should 'get a bloody haircut'. The soldier, Cedric Mays, recovered and became one of Wintle's lifelong friends. He later recalled that he had been 'afraid to die' after Wintle's earbashing.

also have helped his cause that he was being tried by an army tribunal on a charge relating to the RAF. Wintle then left for the front once more.

After seeing action in the Middle East, he went to France to try and convert Vichy soldiers to the allied cause. He was arrested as a spy. After a failed escape attempt, he once again became dismayed with the standards of his captors, going on hunger strike in protest at their lackadaisical appearance and berating them for surrendering to the Germans. After 13 days the prison officers gave in and agreed to allow Wintle to inspect the guards every morning. Wintle accepted their offer, but informed them that it was half past seven, and he took his tea at seven, so they would start again in the morning. Shortly afterwards he escaped successfully; the commandant of the prison later claimed[10] that the entire garrison at the prison where he had been held went over to the Resistance, inspired by his fortitude and patriotism.

Following the war, the dispute began that would take Wintle to the law lords. He believed that a solicitor called Nye had conned one of his elderly female relatives into leaving him £44,000 in her will. Wintle's methods did not initially follow the Rules of the Supreme Court. His wife talked him out of horsewhipping Nye. Instead, Wintle 'debagged'[11] Nye and took photographs to shame him into returning the cash. As a result Wintle, was imprisoned for six months for assault. He then took the more orthodox route of issuing proceedings to contest the will.

At trial the jury rejected Wintle's accusations, as did the Court of Appeal. Wintle, by now out of funds and hence acting in person, nevertheless won his subsequent appeal to the House of Lords on the ground that the trial judge had not properly conveyed to the jury the burden that rested on Nye to disprove

---

[10] When appearing, somewhat bizarrely, on Wintle's *This is Your Life* programme in 1959. He claimed that many of the guards died in battle as a result, but that they had at least been doing their duty as Wintle would have wished.

[11] That is, forced him to remove his trousers.

the allegations.[1] As well as establishing important principles of the law concerning challenges to wills, the case compelled the Law Society (due to the public outcry) to ban solicitors from drafting wills in their own favour. Wintle later said that it was only in the Lords that he found himself amongst his intellectual equals.

After the case Nye was struck off the roll of solicitors. Wintle, on the other hand, received a jeroboam of champagne from the Bar by way of congratulations for his spirited advocacy. He died only a few years later, in 1966, unchanged to the last.

Afterword

Researching Wintle's life was the most entertaining of all the tasks undertaken for this book. It was a costly exercise as well, since Wintle's autobiography, long out of print, fetches a high price second hand. He was clearly something of a celebrity even in his day (although the modern concept of 'celebrity' would have first confused and then appalled him), appearing on *This Is Your Life* and *Desert Island Discs*. Sadly I have not been able to find any recording of the former, but the latter can be found on the BBC website. Needless to say it is first-rate entertainment: Wintle comes across precisely as one might expect – a ramrod straight Colonel in his manner, but a feisty individualist in his approach to life. He clearly struggles to understand how other people might not see the world in the same way he does. Somewhat predictably, his musical choices are made up of military marching tunes and some well-known classical pieces (including the *Vienna Blood Waltz* by Johann Strauss II).

For his book he chooses a blank one that he can write himself, and for a luxury item he opts for a dog whip, not in anticipation of there being any dogs on his island but just in case some Germans or other reprobates turn up. 'I'm never bored in my own company' he reassures the interviewer when asked if he would find it difficult on the island, offering his experiences in solitary confinement in support of that proposition. Also worth seeking out is the television dramatization of his life, like his

[1] See [1959] 1 All ER 552.

autobiography entitled *The Last Englishman*, and starring Jim Broadbent.

Finally, as someone rather proud of having a number of letters published in *The Times*, I have to pay tribute to Wintle's effort from 1946:

Sir,

I have just written you a long letter.

On reading it over, I have thrown it into the waste paper basket.

Hoping this will meet with your approval,

I am, Sir,

Your obedient Servant,

A. D. Wintle[2]

---

[2] Published in the *New Law Journal*, vol 163, 26 July 2013, p 22.

Behind the Candelabra, in Front of the Bench

A much discussed entry for the *Palme d'Or* in Cannes in 2013 was the Stephen Soderberg film *Behind the Candelabra*, a biopic of the late pianist and entertainer Władziu Valentino Liberace. The film charted the relationship Liberace had with the much younger Scott Thorson from the mid-1970s to the former's death in 1987 from an AIDS-related illness.

In 1982 they separated acrimoniously and Thorson brought a lawsuit known in American parlance as 'palimony' (equivalent to a matrimonial claim between unmarried couples), which was eventually settled for a small fraction of what had been claimed (Thorson later disowned the litigation). It was certainly not Liberace's first experience of the law courts: more than two decades earlier, he had brought a case of his own in England which quickly became a *cause célèbre*.

At that time his star was greatly in the ascendancy: it has been claimed he was the highest-paid entertainer in the world for much of the 1950s–70s. His fame was partly based on his talent as a piano player, but also on his outré costumes and stage persona. As he put it, 'I don't give concerts, I put on a show.'

Liberace's act was not to all tastes, especially those of the more conservative British press. In particular, he attracted the disapproval of William (later Sir William) Connor, a journalist at the *Daily Mirror* who wrote under the byline 'Cassandra'. Connor was certainly unafraid of controversy. In 1945, he had accused P. G. Wodehouse of treason for his wartime broadcasts. On the day of Ruth Ellis' execution in 1955 he had argued passionately against capital punishment. In 1956 he described Liberace as the 'summit of sex' and a 'deadly, winking, sniggering, snuggling, chromium-plated, scent-impregnated, luminous, quivering, giggling, fruit-flavoured, mincing, ice-covered heap of mother love ...' Liberace claimed that the article contained clear inferences that he was homosexual. He brought an action in libel accordingly, the trial finally taking place in 1959.

Then – as now – libel in England was a plaintiff's tort, where often the defendant would end up carrying the burden of proof or doomed to lose either way because of the costs involved. Moreover, in 1959 there was no doubt that any allegation about homosexuality would be libelous. Aside from homosexual acts still being illegal, public attitudes had changed little since the time of Oscar Wilde's not entirely dissimilar libel action against the Marquess of Queensberry discussed in Chapter 2 of this book. But whereas in Wilde's case Queensberry had written explicitly in his infamous note that Wilde was a 'posing somdomite' (sic), Connor had deliberately stopped just short of stating that the star was homosexual. Liberace therefore had to prove the inference.

Among other things he argued that 'fruit' was a well-known colloquial term in America for homosexuality. Connor in response claimed he was unaware of that meaning and therefore any inference had been unintentional.

Reading the article nowadays one struggles to believe anyone might have been in any doubt about its meaning. Perhaps for that reason Connor's claimed ignorance about the meaning of 'fruit' seems to be about all that the *Mirror* relied upon in its defence. Certainly it had nothing like the compelling evidence that Queensberry had been able to deploy against Wilde (actual testimony from claimed former lovers).

The former *Mirror* journalist Revel Barker argued[3] that the *Mirror*'s inept defence stemmed from arrogance, based on its popularity. If so, the *Mirror* failed to take on board two things: first, that Liberace's popularity might well overshadow its own; and secondly, that the *Mirror*'s appeal was unlikely to extend to the judiciary. So it proved: the trial judge, Mr Justice Salmon, did little to hide his contempt for popular journalism in general and the *Mirror* by inclusion, with the sort of *de haut en bas* condescension not unknown amongst the judiciary at the time.

Liberace meanwhile was somewhat concerned by the aged appearance of his counsel, Gilbert Beyfus QC (b 1885). But his fears were unfounded: Beyfus began by describing Connor in terms every bit as biting as those Connor had used on Liberace.

---

[3]   *Crying all the way to the bank* (Revell Barker, 2009).

He went on to deploy *The American Thesaurus of Slang* to rebut Connor's claimed ignorance of the meaning of 'fruit'. Liberace himself robustly denied being homosexual when cross-examined.

All those factors combined to secure victory for Liberace, who was awarded substantial damages. As with many other libel actions, the costs incurred by the defence meant that the *Mirror* was effectively bound to lose from the moment the writ was served. On the other hand, its circulation rose considerably in the wake of the trial, so it might not have wholly regretted Connor's piece. It seems there never was such a thing as bad publicity.

Either way, Liberace was triumphant, famously declaring that he 'cried all the way to the bank' (he had not invented the phrase, though it became associated with him). It was not the only time he sued over homosexual allegations either: throughout his lifetime he remained in the closet and aggressively litigious about any insinuation about his sexuality.

Perhaps justice was not really done, given that Connor's inferences about Liberace's sexuality were factually justified. Then again, justice was not really capable of being done. The whole action stemmed from the public stigma that wrongly attached to homosexuality at the time, which gave Liberace no choice other than to live a lie.[4] The resultant fear he must have lived with would not, one imagines, have been wholly offset by his fame and fortune.[5]

---

[4] I should note that one Tony Palmer, in a letter to *The Times* of 6 June 2013, claimed to have known Liberace and said that he was never depressed by living a lie. Instead, 'nothing about him suggested a tortured soul. Quite the contrary. In spite of being sick, he was still loved by his audience, and he loved them. And that was all that mattered to him.'
Incidentally, Liberace's solicitor, David Jacobs, who was also a closet homosexual, seems to have lived a life just as colourful as his client, if a lot less in the public eye. See Mick Brown, 'The Mystery of David Jacobs, Liberace's lawyer', *Telegraph*, 3 June 2013.
[5] Published in the *New Law Journal*, vol 163, 21 June 2013, p 30.

An Ugly Affair

The inveterate newspaper columnist Julie Burchill is not, to put it mildly, someone afraid of speaking her mind. In 1993, during a famous exchange with the American feminist scholar Camille Paglia, Burchill remarked that Paglia had a 'wop name', called her 'a fucking girl' and concluded with 'Fuck off you crazy old dyke'. So when the *Sunday Times* appointed her as a film reviewer around the same time, it would have known what to expect. Burchill did not disappoint. In a review of the 1994 film *The Age of Innocence*, she wrote that 'film directors, from Hitchcock to Berkoff are notoriously hideous-looking people.'

Nine months later she returned to the same theme, in a review of Kenneth Branagh's *Frankenstein*:

> The Creature is made as a vessel for Waldman's brain, and rejected in disgust when it comes out scarred and primeval. It's a very new look for the Creature – no bolts in the neck or flat-top hairdo – and I think it works; it's a lot like Stephen (sic) Berkoff, only marginally better-looking.

The impugned Berkoff was clearly wounded by Burchill's lack of charity. He complained to the newspaper and, dissatisfied with the response, brought an action for libel.

His writ alleged that the two articles were meant and were understood to mean that he was 'hideously ugly'. A preliminary issue was heard to determine whether that meaning was capable of being defamatory. The judge said:

> I am doubtful whether to call a person 'hideously ugly' exposes that person to ridicule, but I have come to the conclusion that it is likely to lead ordinary reasonable people to shun the plaintiff, despite the fact that being hideously ugly is no reflection on a person's character or good reputation. For that reason, albeit with hesitation, I hold that to call a person 'hideously ugly' is defamatory. If justification is pleaded, that will involve the jury deciding whether the plea is made out.

With all due respect, the last sentence in that quotation – contemplating a jury deciding whether Burchill was justified in calling Berkoff hideously ugly – itself invited ridicule. Unsurprisingly, therefore, the defendants went to the Court of

Appeal. Most surprisingly, their appeal was dismissed, albeit by majority decision rather than unanimously.[6]

One of the majority judges, Lord Justice Neill, began with a consideration of the meaning of 'defamatory'. He surveyed a number of authorities from as far back as *De Libellis Famosis*,[7] and including Lord Atkin's famous speech in *Sim v Stretch*.[8] He concluded that it would be:

> open to a jury to conclude that in the context the remarks about Mr Berkoff gave the impression that he was not merely physically unattractive in appearance but actually repulsive. It seems to me that to say this of someone in the public eye who makes his living, in part at least, as an actor, is capable of lowering his standing in the estimation of the public and of making him an object of ridicule.

Lord Justice Phillips (later the first President of the Supreme Court) delivered a concurring judgment.

Lord Justice Millett, on the other hand, was not amused. In a robust dissent, he wrote that:

> however difficult it may be, we must assume that Miss Julie Burchill might be taken seriously. The question then is: is it defamatory to say of a man that he is 'hideously ugly'?
>
> Mr. Berkoff is a director, actor and writer. Physical beauty is not a qualification for a director or writer. Mr. Berkoff does not plead that he plays romantic leads or that the words complained of impugn his professional ability. In any case, I do not think that it can be defamatory to say of an actor that he is unsuitable to play particular roles ...

He concluded:

> If I have appeared to treat Mr. Berkoff's claim with unjudicial levity it is because I find it impossible to take it seriously. ... I remain of the opinion that the proceedings are as frivolous as Miss Burchill's article. The time of the Court ought not to be taken up with either of them.

---

[6] *Berkoff v Burchill and another*, unreported, Court of Appeal, 31 July 1996.
[7] (1605) 5 Co. Rep. 125.
[8] [1936] 2 All ER 1237.

It is impossible to disagree with Millett LJ, for several reasons. First, Burchill was obviously writing in a sardonic and flippant tone. Secondly, even had she been serious, the appropriate response would have been 'so what?' Thirdly, as Millett LJ put it:

> It is a common experience that ugly people have satisfactory social lives – Boris Karloff is not known to have been a recluse – and it is a popular belief for the truth of which I am unable to vouch that ugly men are particularly attractive to women.

Putting the case at its highest, it amounted to a complaint that 'Julie Burchill called Steven Berkoff ugly'. That was not the sort of issue that called for the attention of the expensive and scarce resource of the law courts. Instead it was a primary school-level insult that should have been treated accordingly.

After all that, the controversy does not seem to have affected either party. Berkoff has continued to have a successful acting and directing career. Burchill for her part has maintained her abrasive ways: in 2013, for example, she attracted controversy with an article pouring scorn on what she saw as oversensitivity by transgender spokespeople (or 'dicks in chicks' clothing' as she called them). The Press Complaints Committee declined to censure her, stating that it 'did not address issues of taste and offence.' Neither should the libel courts.[9]

---

[9]   Published in the *New Law Journal*, vol 163, 5 July 2013, p 22.

'To Sparkle Things Up A Bit'

Faced with salacious facts, judges writing the solemn texts that form judgments of the courts generally have two choices. Either they write a narrative in as bland and neutral fashion as they can manage, or they admit from the outset what readers will make of it, and hence go about things with a sense of humour. Lord Denning was one who usually went for the bland narrative, interspersed with some genuine anger, though he was not above a bit of humour of the saucy postcard variety from time to time. Mr Justice Eady, on the other hand, was a more modern judge who favoured a more modern approach.

As a libel law specialist, Eady J often heard the most salacious cases, and one could almost imagine him biting his tongue in restraint as he set out the facts at the start of each judgment. He presided over the case[10] brought by the Formula One panjandrum Max Mosley, who testified among other things that as his bottom was being shaved by the German prostitutes he had hired he was 'shaking with laughter'. Eady J could not confirm or deny that assertion from the video evidence submitted to the court since, he explained, 'it was not his face that was on display'.

Arguably even more risqué than Mosley's exploits were those of the estranged Mr and Mrs Turner in the case of *Turner v News Group Newspapers Ltd and another*.[11] Mr Turner brought libel proceedings concerning an article in the now defunct newspaper *News of the World*. He sued both the newspaper's owners and Mrs Turner. The material part of the article read:

> THE swinging scene was meant to spice up sultry Arisara Turner's marriage – but ended up wrecking it.
>
> The beautiful photographer (pictured right) was 25 when she was introduced to a circle of middle-class swappers by her businessman husband at a Coventry club.
>
> 'I was nervous and needed Dutch courage', recalled Arisara, who lives in west London.

[10]   *Mosley v News Group Newspapers Ltd* [2008] EWHC 1777 (QB).
[11]   [2005] EWHC 892 (QB).

'But inside I spotted a woman eyeing me up and we ended up in a clinch as my husband watched. He couldn't seem to get enough and it turned me on. (...)

'But he kept pressuring me to have sex with the men too, and that I didn't like – even though they were quite well-to-do people, even policemen and doctors.

'After a while I got fed up with it and decided I didn't want to go any more. That caused furious rows at home and in the end we divorced'.

Mr Turner claimed that the article defamed him, by among other things claiming that he 'is and/or was a swinger and/or a wifeswapper and/or a loser.'

The newspaper group offered to publish a suitable correction and apology and to pay compensation and costs, which Mr Turner accepted. But the parties could not agree on the amount of compensation, and so they went to court to resolve the point.[12] Here Mr Turner faced some difficulty. Like the Marquess of Queensberry all those years earlier with Oscar Wilde, the newspaper group had gone looking for information about the claimant's private life that would, if not destroy his claim, at least reduce the damages payable, by besmirching his reputation.

Eady J described three elements the newspaper adduced to that effect:

i) The involvement of the Claimant and second Defendant (Mrs Turner) in fetish functions at a club in Coventry called Ceasars, which advertises itself as 'the Midlands leading fetish, BDSM and swingers club'. Miss Page[13] tells me that BDSM stands for 'Bondage in Discipline, Dominance and Submission, Sadism and Masochism'.

ii) The very active career of the second Defendant as a model posing for what Miss Page described as 'open leg shots' and

[12] The procedure was under s 3(5) of the Defamation Act 1996, which provided that compensation in the circumstances would be determined on the same principles as damages in an ordinary libel claim.
[13] Adrienne Page QC, the barrister representing the defence. She was instructed by Farrer & Co, a distinguished firm of solicitors who for many years represented the Royal Family, including Queen Elizabeth II.

'girl on girl' poses. The Claimant encouraged her in this career, from which she made a modest albeit tax free income, and acted as her agent.

iii) After the Claimant and the second Defendant initially split up, in 2001, she was 'slagged off' by the Claimant in The Sun newspaper under the title 'Page 3 Thai girl wed me just to get into Britain' and he called for her deportation.

To prove the second of those elements, the newspaper submitted a portfolio of Mrs Turner's professional pictures. Eady J explained:

> The next subject is that of the explicit photographs. ... It seems that Mrs Turner was something of a 'trooper' in this enterprise. She appeared on an X-rated Adult Channel, and in magazines such as Men Only, Men's World, Mayfair, For Men, International Park Lane, and Asian Babes. Thousands of photographs were taken and some video material, of which I was provided with a selection in evidence.
>
> Mrs Turner was happy, time and again, to go on displaying her perineum from every possible angle. She pulled her labia about to give the viewer opportunities for quasigynaecological inspection. In many shots she had a ring inserted at the upper end of her labia. This was no doubt to sparkle things up a bit and also perhaps to give her better purchase. She is shown, for example, in some photographs using it like a ringpull. There were also photographs of other women, with whom she was rolling about naked. (...)
>
> According to the Claimant, Mrs Turner enjoyed her work: there was no question of his 'pressuring' her to do it. She was keen to have a measure of independence by making some spending money for herself (free of tax).

Taking all those factors into account, Eady J decided to reduce the damages recoverable by 40%. He awarded Mr Turner the net sum of £9,000. The newspaper group appealed unsuccessfully to the Court of Appeal, which held that Eady J had not applied the law incorrectly or otherwise erred. I leave it to readers to decide whether Mr Turner's victory was worth the effort on his part.

Snake Oil

The great American physicist Richard Feynman used to have a lot of fun at the expense of what he called 'cargo cult science': purported scientific claims involving unjustifiable conclusions drawn from poor observation or selective premises. Sadly, although our understanding of the world has advanced considerably since Feynman's premature death in 1988, there seems to be just as much cargo cult science around as ever.[14] Worse, Britain's claimant-friendly libel laws have sometimes been employed by the cargo cultists to evade or deflect scrutiny.

Fortunately, a few genuine scientists have still been prepared to risk litigation in order to subject cultish claims to proper scrutiny. I have previously written of Dr Simon Singh, who managed to face down an attempt by the British Chiropractic Association to silence his criticisms via the law courts.[15] Another brave campaigner for truth in the 21st century, and an enthusiastic disciple of Feynman, is Dr Ben Goldacre, author of the invaluable book *Bad Science*[16] and a newspaper column of the same name. In 2014, an amusing exchange he had on Twitter with one of the targets of his book gave rise to threats of litigation, but instead ended in something approaching humiliation for his antagonist and a victory for both free speech and common sense.

The target in question was the television personality Gillian McKeith. She held herself out to be an expert on nutrition and for a time called herself 'Dr Gillian McKeith PhD'. Dr Goldacre was unimpressed. In *Bad Science*, he took apart a number of her original claims about nutrition. He pointed out that some

---

[14] The worst example is probably homeopathy, which manages to receive public funds in the United Kingdom despite the absurdity of its premise and the total lack of scientific support for its claimed efficacy. See Melissa Davey, 'Homeopathy not effective for treating any condition, Australian report finds', *The Guardian*, 11 March 2015, http://www.theguardian.com/lifeandstyle/2015/mar/11/homeopathy-not-effective-for-treating-any-condition-australian-report-finds (Retrieved 11 March 2015).
[15] See *Cases, Causes and Controversies*, Chapter 21.
[16] Harper Perennial, 2007.

were preposterous, such as the idea that photosynthesis might take place in the digestive tract. (Since photosynthesis requires sunlight, anyone whose intestines were exposed in that fashion would have more immediate problems than poor nutrition.) Her more valid arguments were mostly anodyne and unoriginal – along the lines of eating more vegetables and exercising more.

As to McKeith herself, Dr Goldacre pointed out that that both the 'university' from which she obtained her nutritional qualification (she had legitimate unrelated qualifications from a different institution) and the 'professional body' to which she belonged were not of any academic or professional standing. McKeith objected until Dr Goldacre obtained membership of the same professional body for his dead cat.

Thereafter McKeith stopped claiming to have a PhD but nevertheless carried on selling her remedies and advice. Then, in 2010, she tweeted that Goldacre's book was 'lies about another by an ass who makes money from pharmaceutical giants.'[17]

As the lawyer David Allen Green pointed out at the time,[18] McKeith's tweet was *prima facie* libellous. It would certainly have passed the classic definition of libel of lowering the claimant's reputation in the minds of right-thinking people generally. Not surprisingly, therefore, Dr Goldacre challenged McKeith, tweeting back 'hi @gillianmckeith, i'm writing a piece about you libelling me in the context of #libelreform, can you pls contact ben@badscience.net thnks'.

In Dr Goldacre's words, this is what happened next:[19]

@gillianmckeith's Twitter feed was filled with the abuse of a random passing Twitterer, and long tweets explaining how Dr McKeith's PhD from a non-accredited correspondence college was entirely valid. Then they all disappeared. The tone shifted: instead of first person stuff about Gillian's life and family, lots of third person PR tweets appeared. Then they disappeared.

---

[17] http://www.theweek.co.uk/politics/13203/vanishing-tweets-reignite-mckeith-goldacre-war#ixzz3DkwqByly'.

[18] Ibid.

[19] 'Ben Goldacre: why I'm battling it out with Gillian McKeith again', *Guardian*, 18 July 2010, http://www.theguardian.com/science/2010/jul/18/ben-goldacre-gillian-mckeith-twitter.

> Then, as more than 1,000 people were tweeting about her, making it the top trending topic on Twitter, @gillianmckeith announced 'do you really believe this is real Twitter site for the GM?'

> Yes, replied the geeks. The Twitter account @gillianmckeith is linked to gillianmckeith.info, explained some. Then that link was deleted. Ah, explained others: only half-deleted. If you look at the 'source code' for the page, the link is there, just temporarily inactivated. And that Twitter account is still linked from gillianmckeith.tv, Gillian's YouTube page. Yes, we believe this is the real Twitter site for the real Gillian McKeith. So if you're going to play silly buggers online, at least do it competently.

He also pointed out that he could sue for libel, but chose not to, preferring the marketplace of ideas.

If McKeith's credentials and her 'work' had been genuine, both could have been proved, to the satisfaction of all her critics, with little or no effort on her part and certainly no need for libel threats or abuse.[20] Her qualifications could have been verified within short order if they had been obtained from a proper educational institute. And the research for her books would have been recorded in established, refereed journals, or at least published with all assumptions and potential errors declared up front. Instead, at the time of writing, no such justification has been forthcoming and her research on nutrition has never been published in a reputable scientific journal.

Dr Goldacre's efforts have not been in vain, as can be gauged by the fact that McKeith has not followed through on any threat to sue her now quite numerous critics. But it remains the case that fear of the cost, uncertainty and general hassle from litigation under Britain's overly claimant-friendly libel laws must have given critics pause for thought for all the wrong reasons.

The frustrating thing is that, rather than following unqualified advice, people could instead read the work of genuine scientists

---

[20] See Ben Goldacre, 'What's wrong with Gillian McKeith?', *The Guardian*, 12 February 2007, http://www.theguardian.com/media/2007/feb/12/advertising.food.

such as Drs Singh and Goldacre and the much-missed Professor Feynman. Not only would they find better science, they would enjoy a much more interesting and entertaining read as well.

War Horse

In one episode of the original *Muppets* television show, the band tires of the theme tune, believing it to be 'too square', and decides to quit. Kermit tries to persuade them to stay. Negotiations on the band's behalf are led by the bass player, Floyd Pepper. After a time, Floyd announces that they will stay, but only on condition he can write the new theme himself, prompting the following exchange:

Kermit: 'Oh that'll be fine with me'

Floyd: 'No it won't man'

Kermit: 'Why not?'

Floyd: 'You hate my music. You wouldn't understand my music ... Nobody understands my music. I mean, I don't even understand it. If I didn't know I was a genius, I wouldn't listen to the trash I write'.

Floyd is proved to have a point when the band plays his composition, *Fugue for Frog*. Kermit naturally loves the title, but the actual music turns out to be an appalling farrago resembling the worst efforts of Frank Zappa or Captain Beefheart.

Eventually, all seems to be resolved off camera, since the band returns as normal in the following episode. But it is a nice illustration of a dispute with legal connotations involving competing artistic visions. A not dissimilar real-world example appeared early in 2014, when the National Theatre found itself in court after dispensing with some of its contracted musicians for one of the best-known plays of the past decade, *War Horse*. The case was *Ashworth and others v The Royal National Theatre*.[21]

War Horse, which was based on a children's book by Michael Morpurgo, was immensely successful, both critically and commercially. No less than Steven Spielberg purchased the rights and turned it into a feature film. For the English stage production, a mixture of recorded music and live performances

---

[21]   [2014] EWHC 1176 (QB).

was originally used, but for all overseas productions only recorded music was employed. After a time, for a number of reasons – not solely cost-related – the English producers decided they too would only use recorded music. They therefore gave notice to the musicians.

The musicians were very upset, and refused to accept the rejection. Instead, in a somewhat bathetic scene, they arrived at the theatre ready to appear the next scheduled performance, but were turned away. They then issued proceedings for unfair dismissal and applied for an injunction requiring them to be reinstated pending resolution of the claim at trial.

Their case turned on the interpretation of the contracts in question, which were based on standard-form agreements common to West End productions. I would observe that it is not very satisfactory from a legal point of view that the contracts were so ambiguously worded as to give rise to a dispute over the permissible means of termination. It was not a case where there was disagreement over the facts; it was purely a dispute over the wording of the contracts. Since they were the same agreements which had been in use in a number of productions over many years, one would have thought that the basic provisions including (or especially) those relating to termination would have been put beyond reasoned disagreement long before.[22]

That aside, the interesting aspect of the claim was the injunction that the claimants sought. If granted, it would have entailed the court overriding the artistic wishes of the producers and forcing (at least temporarily) the return of the musicians. Usually, artists who consider they have wrongly terminated from a contract only sue for damages, calculated primarily by the amount they expected to earn from their performances. Courts would not order the contract to be performed, because it would risk the unwilling party trying to ruin the services.

---

[22] In international shipping, for example, there are a number of documents such as bills of lading and charterparties which have been in use for many decades, and of which virtually every clause has been litigated to death, meaning legal disputes are extremely rare.

In Kermit's case, for example, the band might have been in breach of contract for walking out without prior notice. If so, Kermit could sue and recover damages. But if he was also able to get an order for specific performance requiring the band to continue playing, they would probably try and play the theme tune so badly (or slip in *Fugue for Frog* at every possible moment) that they would spoil the show. Kermit might try and sue them again, but then the court would have to decide whether the band really had played badly (rather than just 'creatively'), and needless to say judges are not best placed to determine the merits of fugues for frogs or anyone else. Nor is it a subject on which one could really take expert evidence, since opinions on music vary so wildly.

For a real-world example, the progressive rock band *The Alan Parsons Project* was once compelled by their record company to make an album against their wishes; they responded with a collection of strange noises they entitled *The Sicilian Defence* (in reference to the well-known chess strategy). None of the songs on the album was released until decades later.[23]

The *War Horse* musicians argued that there would not be a problem in their case, since they were professionals; they had performed the roles in the play for years without criticism; they were familiar with the arrangements and capable of adapting their performances in line with any alternations in artistic direction; the other actors would welcome them back; and only limited rehearsals would be necessary. They conceded, however, that the National Theatre could require them to play simply one note under the terms of the contract, if it was determined to exclude them from the play.

The basis of the National Theatre's defence was that the producers considered that the play was better without the musicians. That was a matter of artistic judgement, with which the courts could not interfere.

---

[23]   It might be argued that the outcome of the great actress Bette Davis' case against Warner Bros was no different, because the reality was that Davis could not earn the same money except by returning to America to make films against her wishes. See *Cases, Causes and Controversies*, Chapter 5.

The judge came down firmly on the side of the National Theatre. He agreed that the exclusion of the live musicians was a question of artistic judgement and therefore not something with which the court could interfere. It was, he said:

> precisely the type of situation where on the authorities it would be inappropriate for the court to enforce a contract by specific performance or analogous injunction. There is clearly an absence of personal confidence on the part of the National Theatre. In addition the claimants themselves would be affected by knowing that the National Theatre does not want them and believes that the play is better without them.

He also held that damages would be an adequate remedy if the claimants were to establish that they had been dismissed in breach of contract.

There can be no great surprise at the judge's decision. Rather unfortunately, one of the reasons for the claim seems to have been the musicians' concern about a loss of performing kudos. One doubts that that is something the courts could have done anything about, however they might have decided the case.

A Greyer Shade of Grey?

The *War Horse* case was but one of a myriad number of cases involving musicians in one form or another. In its final batch of judgments before re-branding itself as the Supreme Court, the House of Lords allowed the appeal of the keyboard player Matthew Fisher against a former member of the band Procol Harum and their record company. Fisher claimed joint-authorship of the band's best-known song *A Whiter Shade of Pale*,[24] on the ground that he had been responsible for the organ heard in the song. The trial judge agreed and, although the Court of Appeal allowed the appeal of the defendants, that finding of fact was never challenged.

The decision about the musical composition was fairly straightforward. Fisher had the idea for, and the execution of, the organ part, which was unquestionably an integral part of the famous version of the song, and therefore he was entitled to a share of the royalties. But there were two wrinkles in the equation: first, Fisher admitted he had heavily borrowed from Bach in the composition of the organ part. Secondly, since he had waited decades before bringing the claim, with no good reason for the delay, he was only entitled for a cut of royalties from the point of the claim, not backdated to the composition of the song, which reduced the monetary value of his victory very considerably.

A similar action a few years earlier concerned the Bluebells' song *Young at Heart*. Different versions of the song had been released since the early 1980s, but without much chart success until it was used in a Volkswagen advertisement in the early 1990s. The question in the case was whether the distinctive fiddle sound introduced in a later version entitled the fiddle player (the session musician Bobby Valentino) to be considered a joint-composer of the successful version of the song (it did, according to the Chancery Division).[25]

---

[24] *Fisher v Brooker and others* [2009] UKHL 41.
[25] *Beckingham v Hodgens and others* [2002] All ER (D) 24 (Jul). A subsequent appeal was dismissed.

This is an area of law that is not particularly cut and dried. The legal test for entitlement to royalties for records necessarily involves the somewhat esoteric question of what constitutes a song at all. Ordinarily, a song is considered to consist of lyrics and the melody, and whoever is responsible for those would be considered the composer or composers. Immediately one can single out *A Whiter Shade of Pale* as an exception, given that Fisher had written neither. In some cases the riff would be seen as the signature of the tune, particularly in the genre of classic rock: Deep Purple's *Smoke on the Water* and Led Zeppelin's *Whole Lotta Love* (familiar to anyone who remembers the television programme *Top of the Pops*) are two obvious examples. In traditional blues music, many of the classic 12-bar arrangements tend to be generic and it would be impossible to agree on their origins, save for the point that, even if the original composer or composers could be identified, they would have been dead for many decades and therefore their copyright would have expired years ago.

More difficult still is virtually the entire body of music that is jazz. In most live performances there is a significant degree of improvisation. To take just one example, the most famous part of Duke Ellington's band's rendition at the 1956 Newport Jazz Festival of his original work *Diminuendo and Crescendo in Blue* was a saxophone solo by Paul Gonsalves, which was almost completely improvised. Should Gonsalves, rather than – or at least as well as – Ellington therefore be considered the composer of the piece?

What of the famous scat singing by Ella Fitzgerald or Cab Calloway? In the related genre of blues, Robert Johnson songs have been covered countless times, by Eric Clapton and others. Clapton, as far as I am aware, has never claimed to be a composer or joint-composer of any of them, and is not listed as such in the liner notes to the albums or CDs in which they appear. Yet, in many cases, Clapton's versions of the songs are much more sophisticated, and sometimes almost unrecognisable as the same song. Should, therefore, any such songs be considered his, and those parts borrowed from Johnson purely incidental?

(That said, Johnson is often reputed to have sold his soul to the Devil in exchange for his musical gift, so perhaps Clapton has been erring on the side of caution least he provoke an irate response from the actual original composer.[26])

Once one reaches the 1980s and the era of sampling, then at once the issue becomes both more difficult and easier at the same time. If someone has lifted an entire part of an earlier recording then it is hard not to say that the original person should receive the credit – MC Hammer's appropriation of Rick James's *Superfreak* for his 1990 song *Can't Touch This*, for example. Then again, one would have to judge how much the sampled part actually formed part of the later work.

Another controversial example is The Verve's *Bittersweet Symphony*, which drew on an orchestral version of The Rolling Stones' song, *The Last Time*, and led to the latter's record company demanding all of the royalties (instead of an apparent earlier agreement to share them).

Then there is the issue of producers. George Martin has occasionally been known as the 'Fifth Beatle' in recognition of his contribution to the band's music and how it developed through the 1960s, and his contemporary Phil Spector's 'Wall of Sound' went substantially towards creating a style of music familiar for decades afterwards. In later years, the likes of Nile Rodgers, Mike Chapman, Pete Waterman and others have at times been so influential in the sound of the bands for whom they have been responsible that it seems to me that they should be credited as composers.

Returning to the legal definition of song composition, the short answer is that in almost all instances the matter is resolved by contract before the recording is even made. Hence, of the millions of pop songs, only very few have provoked litigation. Aspirant composers would therefore be well advised to exercise caution before signing on the dotted line.

---

[26] The rumour actually started in respect of another singer, Tommy Johnson, and it seems was later modified to refer to Robert Johnson instead. *Wikipedia* at the time of writing had quite a well-researched and referenced article on the subject.

Afterword

After I had drafted the above, it was reported that the children of Marvin Gaye, who inherited the rights to his music, had successfully brought an action in America claiming that the Robin Thicke song *Blurred Lines* (primarily written by Pharrell Williams) had borrowed too heavily from their late father's 1977 song *Got to Give it Up*.[27] The decision was made by a jury, who, unlike judges, do not have to give reasons for their decisions. Readers are therefore invited to listen to both songs and form their own view.[28]

---

[27] 'Blurred Lines jury awards Marvin Gaye family $7m', *BBC News*, 11 March 2015, http://www.bbc.co.uk/news/entertainment-arts-31825059 (Retrieved 11 March 2015). The damages were later reduced on appeal.

[28] For further reading, an interesting place to start is Clinton Heylin, *It's One For The Money: How Song Snatchers Carved Up A Century Of Pop* (Constable & Robinson, 2015), published shortly before this book went to press.

Plagiarise ... Let No One Else's Work Evade Your Eyes ...

It is not often that the celebrated American singer, pianist and mathematics teacher Tom Lehrer is quoted in court. A special commendation should therefore be given to Mr Justice Males, who began his judgment in *R (on the application of Mustafa) v Office of the Independent Adjudicator, Queen Mary College Interested Party*[29] with the words 'The Harvard academic and songwriter Tom Lehrer recommended plagiarism as the route to academic success, wealth and fame, but his tongue was firmly in his cheek.' Males J was referring to Lehrer's *Lobachevsky*:

> Plagiarize
>
> Let no one else's work evade your eyes
>
> Remember why the good Lord made your eyes
>
> So don't shade your eyes
>
> But plagiarize, plagiarize, plagiarize
>
> Only be sure always to call it please 'research'

Males J might also have mentioned Stephen Fry's novel *The Liar*, in which the curmudgeonly Professor Trefusis lavishes praise on a student's essay, finishing with a final compliment that it 'must have taken almost an hour to copy out.' He consoles the student by pointing out that even if the student had managed an original essay, he would still have had to read it, and he would far rather read the excellent copied essay than any inferior original effort the student might have produced.

But the case before Males J was, as he acknowledged, no laughing matter. It raised an interesting question of general importance, namely whether plagiarism is a question of academic judgement, only for universities to decide, or whether an independent body or the courts could intervene. In the internet age, with so much information available to students so easily (who, unlike those in Trefusis's day, can cut and paste

---

[29]   [2013] EWHC 1379 (Admin).

in a matter of seconds) the question is a very pressing one for teachers and academics.

The claim concerned a student, Hazim Mustafa, at Queen Mary College in London. He was undertaking a Master's degree in project management. As part of the course he submitted an essay on the 'risk management of a large technology based project'. He was awarded zero marks for the essay, on the ground that some of it was plagiarised. Aggrieved by the decision, he appealed unsuccessfully via the university's internal processes, and eventually made a complaint to the Office of the Independent Adjudicator (OIA). He did not deny using third party material in his essay. Rather, the issue was whether or not he had done so with proper attribution. The OIA rejected the complaint on the ground that the existence (and if so, the extent) of plagiarism was a matter of academic judgment, which was a matter purely for the university. Mustafa then challenged that decision in the courts, by way of an application for judicial review.

The issue before the court was 'whether the determination of plagiarism is necessarily a matter of judgment and so always outside the OIA's jurisdiction'. A secondary question was whether the OIA was correct that a decision as to penalty following a finding of plagiarism was not a matter of academic judgment and therefore immune from review. Say, for example, a university decided that 5% of one essay had been plagiarised, but that essay was only worth 10% of the total mark for a course, the question might arise whether it was proportionate for the student to be held to have failed the entire course. Would that be a decision purely of academic judgment, or could the OIA interfere if it felt the university was too heavy-handed?

The judge reviewed some authorities and concluded:

> To my mind, it is reasonably clear that the question whether plagiarism has been committed often (and perhaps usually) will require an exercise of academic judgment, but that it need not necessarily do so. Take the case, for example, where a student lifts wholesale an article from the internet which he presents as his own work without attribution or other acknowledgement. The computer programme will demonstrate 100% copying and no judgment is required, academic or otherwise, in order to

determine that there has been plagiarism. It may be that such a case will be referred to an academic to decide what to do, but that will be a decision on what to do about the plagiarism and not a determination whether plagiarism has taken place – or even if it is, it is not a determination which requires any exercise of judgment.

In other words, in the majority of cases, the question would be solely one for the university in question, but not always: it would not always require specialist knowledge to work out that someone has cut and pasted something. On the other hand, in such obvious cases, it would be much less likely that there could be a dispute and therefore much less likely that anyone would be trying to appeal to the OIA or thereafter to a court.

Males J held that it was not necessary to decide whether a decision on penalty was a matter of academic judgment. He expressly stated that he wished to reserve his view for another day.

Given that Males J had decided that some cases of plagiarism could fall outside pure academic judgment and be the subject of challenge before the OIA, the question thus arose as to whether Mustafa's complaint was such a case. The judge held that it was not, and he therefore dismissed the claim. But he added a small qualification by way of mitigation, by pointing out that the case did not involve any 'moral turpitude' on Mustafa's part. All that had happened was that Mustafa had failed properly to indicate which parts of his essay were transposed.

Afterword

A friend of mine of many years standing is the New Zealand philosopher Dr Simon Clarke. In 2014 he suspected that an essay from one of his students had been written by a company that brazenly offered to write essays for a fee. He has permitted me to reproduce the following exchange he had with the company via its online customer service facility. It makes for illuminating reading:

Mary (08:02:44): Hi Simon, how may I help you?

Simon (08:02:37): On your webpage, you say 'Here you can hire an independent writer/researcher to custom write you an authentic essay to your specifications that will pass any plagiarism test (e.g. Turnitin)'

Simon (08:02:41): Is that true?

Mary (08:03:23): Yes, that is true Simon.

Simon (08:03:17): Don't you think that is encouraging students to cheat?

Mary (08:04:10): In our opinion, there is nothing unethical about asking for help. When you order an essay online, you realize that maybe you need more academic support to successfully complete your studies. Deciding to buy a term paper is the same as deciding to hire a tutor. You are not doing anything wrong by looking for a reasonable solution to your academic problems.

Simon (08:04:14): Tutors do not write papers for their students.

Mary (08:05:30): Our clients will be able to see how their papers needs (sic) to be written and customize it based on how they want their paper written.

Simon (08:05:34): I'm a professor. I got to your website because Turnitin has picked up one of my students plagiarising her essay from your site.

Mary (08:08:31): You can send us the paper and we can take a look at it.

Simon (08:09:08): I think it is a good service to help students by giving suggestions. But writing papers for them does not help them. They just submit the paper (cheating) and they have not learnt anything themselves. You're harming students and undermining education systems.

Mary (08:10:33): We do understand that. We thank you for your insight.

Simon (08:13:26): Will my comments make any difference, Mary?

Mary (08:15:24): We actually advise client's (sic) to not submit the paper 'as is'. It's mentioned on our terms of service 'You agree that the written material produced represents a model work that should not be submitted for academic credit 'as is'. You may use the work for further research or may edit it to match your writing style, level and vocabulary. We do not guarantee any specific letter grades or any other form of academic approval and can only guarantee to provide quality work based on the original order description.'

Simon (08:16:01): Ok, well that's something I guess. No way to enforce it though. How do you know students don't just go ahead and submit the essays 'as is'?

Mary (08:16:59): We have no control of that but we have advised them on the website.

Simon (08:20:57): It's like selling a gun to a known killer but saying 'we advise you not to use it.'

Mary (08:22:40): We don't see it that way Simon.

Simon (08:23:25): What's the difference (other than the seriousness of the harm of course)? In principle, they are similar.

Mary (08:25:00): Well we do know that the client's (sic) are going to use the paper. We just advise them that it can be used as a reference or teach them how to properly write (sic).

Simon (08:26:06): To teach them how to properly write, you can give them essays on completely different topics. To give them a reference, you could give them references (ie suggest books and articles).

Mary (08:27:31): We also offer that kind of service. It depends on what the client needs us to do.

Simon (08:29:35): Needs or wants? There seems no reason to write an essay for them, except to give them something to submit.

Mary (08:31:28): Our business caters to what our client needs Simon. Thank you for understanding.

Simon (08:33:46): Well, I don't think I do understand, except that the service just writes essays for students in exchange for money.

Mary (08:35:50): We do understand we're (sic) you're coming from.

Simon (08:37:47): Thanks for your time.

Mary (08:38:50): You're welcome.

I would first observe that 'Mary', if she is responsible for her own posts, could take some lessons on grammar, or perhaps she should pay someone else to write her pieces for her. Secondly, it seems to me that the saga is an example of how the internet, in many respects the greatest educational tool in history, can also lend itself to intellectual impoverishment.

Part VIII: Public Law

This section has two very different cases I have put together under the heading of 'public law', namely law relating to the organs of the state and the relations between the government and its citizens.

The Erebus case was probably the most difficult of all the articles in this book to write, mostly because of the sheer volume of material written on the disaster. The reports by Chippendale and Mahon, together with the judgments of the Court of Appeal and Privy Council are the minimum required reading for anyone interested in the matter. The Mahon report is superbly written but, at least in the technical description of how the aircraft worked, not a particularly light read.

On top of those official documents are any number of books and articles by lawyers, journalists and others. In recent times, a controversial New Zealand journalist, the late Paul Holmes, produced a 170,000 word book entitled *Daughters of Erebus*.[1] I am afraid to say that his work has to be taken with considerable caution. Much of it is a worthy and genuine tribute to the family whom Captain Collins left behind. No one can have anything other than the highest sympathy for them and the other relatives of the dead crew. But Holmes announced right from his prologue that he had made his mind up, stating that he had 'not consulted' anyone who he thought might agree with Chippendale or otherwise disagree with Mahon. His arguments are therefore vulnerable to a charge of bias.

As I have concluded in the article, the strong disagreement that exists not simply amongst journalists and other lay people but between highly distinguished pilots means that the court of public opinion will never lay the matter to rest.

There can be no disagreement about the magnitude of the wrongdoing involved in the second essay in this part, concerning

---

[1] Hodder Moa, 2011.

voter fraud in the United Kingdom. Vote-rigging threatens the very basis of democratic government, as goes without saying, and therefore one would expect any sign of it to attract a swift and decisive response from the authorities. Regrettably, there was nothing of the sort, only complete apathy, for many years after the first instance was uncovered.

'... an orchestrated litany of lies'

No judicial officer ever wishes to be compelled to say that he has listened to evidence which is false. He always prefers to say, as I hope the hundreds of judgments which I have written will illustrate, that he cannot accept the relevant explanation, or that he prefers a contrary version set out in the evidence.

But in this case, the palpably false sections of evidence which I heard could not have been the result of mistake, or faulty recollection. They originated, I am compelled to say, in a pre-determined plan of deception. They were very clearly part of an attempt to conceal a series of disastrous administrative blunders and so ... I am forced reluctantly to say that I had to listen to an orchestrated litany of lies.

Hon. Justice Mahon

On 28 November 1979, Air New Zealand Flight 901 departed New Zealand for a non-stop sightseeing tour over the frozen wastes of Antarctica. It was flown by two experienced pilots, Captain Jim Collins and First Officer Greg Cassin.

Although not within the terms agreed by the airline with the civil aviation authorities, it was common practice on Antarctic sightseeing flights for pilots to descend below the minimum safe altitude of 16,000 ft if the conditions allowed. Indeed, Air New Zealand advertised as much in its publications. Thus, shortly after arriving in Antarctica, Captain Collins brought the aircraft down to 1,500 ft. He had been offered a radar-controlled descent to that height by the air traffic controllers at the American McMurdo airbase ('McMurdo'), but opted instead to perform his own descent.

Not having flown in Antarctica before, Collins was relying primarily on the aircraft's internal navigation computer system (AINS) – a normally failsafe method of proceeding on a pre-determined path. Visibility was apparently good and thus all seemed well. But no one on board had any idea that two malign factors were about to combine in a catastrophic fashion. First, the wrong co-ordinates had been entered by the ground crew into the AINS system, placing it miles away from where the pilots had been briefed they were to fly. Instead of proceeding down a path over flat sea ice, as the crew all assumed, the AINS system was in fact taking the aircraft directly towards Mt Erebus, the highest peak in the region.

Secondly, the pilots were experiencing the polar phenomenon known as 'sector whiteout', in which perfectly dry snow tricks unsuspecting pilots into thinking they are flying over flat terrain when they are in fact headed towards the side of a snow-covered mountain.

All was calm on the flight deck until the ground proximity radar sounded a warning. Collins gave the order to 'go around power', but it was too late. Seconds later the aircraft collided with Mt Erebus, killing everyone on board instantly.

Back in New Zealand, with no radio contact for many hours, it eventually reached the point where the aircraft had to have run out of fuel, and a shattered chief executive, Morrie Davies, announced the loss. A day later the wreckage was found by search and rescue from McMurdo. The New Zealand Chief Inspector of Air Accidents, Ron Chippendale, began a statutory inquiry immediately. His report a few weeks later blamed the pilots for proceeding at a low altitude in conditions of 'poor visibility' when the crew was 'uncertain' about their position. But, before Chippendale had even submitted his report, the Government established a Royal Commission of Inquiry, headed by a single judge, Peter Mahon, widely considered one of New Zealand's finest legal minds.

Mahon's report, published over a year after the accident, was a masterpiece of formal prose: pithy, incisive and eloquent in equal measure. In complete contrast to Chippendale, Mahon wholly exonerated the pilots, instead blaming the airline: '[T] he single dominant and effective cause of the disaster was the mistake made by those airline officials who programmed the aircraft to fly directly at Mt Erebus and omitted to tell the aircrew'.

Mahon also noted the accident would not have taken place without the 'malevolent trick of the polar light' in the form of sector whiteout.

But that was not all. Mahon went on to issue a brutal denunciation of the airline's conduct before the inquiry. It amounted, he said, to 'an orchestrated litany of lies' – a phrase that swiftly entered the New Zealand vernacular. He imposed a heavy costs order on the airline, clearly intended as punishment for their lack of co-operation with the inquiry. That denunciation led to the matter ending up in the courts, as perhaps had been inevitable all along given the magnitude of the disaster.

The legal proceedings were begun by the airline executives, who had resigned once the report had been issued. They applied for judicial review of the report. The restrictions under New Zealand law at the time meant that they could not challenge the judge's conclusions concerning the cause of the crash. But they were able to challenge his findings that there had been a conspiracy to cover the airline's tracks and his decision to impose a costs award.

Unusually, though sensibly in the circumstances, the case began in the Court of Appeal rather than the High Court. All five judges were sharply critical of Mahon J. They noted somewhat begrudgingly the fact that they could not challenge his findings about causation, but resoundingly rejected his finding of a cover-up. In particular, they held: (i) that Mahon had failed to comply with natural justice by not putting the accusations to witnesses during their evidence, and (ii) that the evidence did not establish a conspiracy anyway. The costs award was therefore quashed and the airline's executives cleared of blame for their post-crash conduct.

A mortified Mahon resigned as a judge and appealed to the Privy Council in London, bringing the final legal stage to the opposite side of the world from where the wreckage of Flight 901 still lay.

The Privy Council began by praising the 'brilliance' of Mahon's work. They too noted that no challenge to the findings of causation was possible. Unlike the Court of Appeal, however, they stated emphatically that there had been 'ample evidence' supporting Mahon's conclusions about the cause of the crash and the blame.

Nevertheless, they went on to reject Mahon's appeal. They agreed with the Court of Appeal that Mahon had breached natural justice because some key witnesses had not been given the opportunity to answer the case ultimately made against them. They accepted that some false testimony might have been presented, but said it was the responsibility of individual witnesses, and not the result of a company conspiracy.

The result of the legal saga, therefore, was that the pilots were absolved of blame as far as the accident was concerned, but the airline was off the hook for its behaviour during the inquiry.

Not many were happy with that outcome. The pilots' supporters did not like the confusion and suspicion that arose from the two court rulings criticising the judge, while the airline was left with the findings of fault for the accident itself. Far from ending the controversy, therefore, the legal rulings gave grist to a still-grinding mill.

Many years later the Mahon report was finally tabled before Parliament, Air New Zealand gave a formal apology to the victims of the accident, and the names of Mahon and Collins were used for airline safety awards.[2] All those developments pointed towards Mahon's conclusions gaining official acceptance. But it would be fair to say that the court of public opinion has never delivered a final verdict, and there is still a body of expert opinion which blames the pilots.

As Mahon noted, there were a number of steps in the chain of causation and if any single one had been removed, the accident would not have occurred. It seems to me that the airline has to bear primary responsibility, for at least three reasons. First, it permitted – even encouraged – flying below the minimum safe altitude, thereby introducing an element of risk which has no place in the world of commercial airliners.

Secondly, the airline sent a crew with almost no experience of the region. Though the science of sector whiteout was not fully understood at the time, the existence of special challenges

---

[2] For further reading, see the extensive resources on this website: http://www.erebus.co.nz/.

in polar flying certainly was. Moreover, a crew experienced in Antarctica would have been familiar with the landmarks and thus able to spot that something was amiss.

Thirdly – and most importantly – is the error identified by Mahon as the overriding factor, namely the changing of the co-ordinates by the airline without informing the crew.

Pace Mahon, however, it does not necessarily follow that the pilots should be wholly exonerated. Some experts argue that Captain Collins was in the wrong for not relying on sources other than AINS and for making his own descent rather than a radar-controlled descent under the direction of McMurdo.[3] Others say he should have ignored the company's tolerance of low-altitude flying. And so the debate continues.

---

[3] See for example the article by Captain Derek Ellis, a retired Concorde pilot, in the *New Zealand Herald* on 13 March 2012.

Shaming a Banana Republic

Democracy is the cornerstone of the British system of government, and it goes without saying that democracy relies on a corruption-free voting system. Corrupt democracy, as shown by countless reprehensible regimes around the world for many years, is no democracy at all. Democracy is probably the one basic principle of public law that would gain unanimous public understanding and approval.

It was therefore a shock to find three cases from England in the 21st century concerning what a judge of the Electoral Court called vote rigging on 'an industrial scale'. Almost as shocking as the corruption itself was the supine response which each of the three cases received from the authorities.

The three cases were all heard in the Electoral Court before Commissioner (Judge) Mawrey QC. The first case was in 2005. It is usually referred to as the 'Birmingham judgment'.[4] Judge Mawrey found that there had been extensive electoral fraud in the two wards concerned (and in all probability in a number of other Birmingham wards), by which the candidates in question and their associates had falsified literally thousands of votes to secure election to the City Council. In exasperation, Judge Mawrey said 'short of writing "STEAL ME" on the envelopes, it is hard to see what more could be done to ensure their coming into the wrong hands'.

The opportunity for the fraud had arisen because of the introduction of postal voting on demand. The judge identified no fewer than 14 different ways in which the system could be successfully defrauded. He observed the view that the situation was by no means confined to Birmingham or confined to members of the particular ethnic minority involved. The problem was universal and had the potential to undermine the democratic process.

---

[4]   Petition M/307/04 (Aston), M/309/04 (Bordesley Green): judgment reported at [2005] All ER (D) 15. Judgment affirmed by the Divisional Court [2005] EWHC 2365 (Admin).

The judge turned to the state of the law and attacked the official Government statement which had claimed that the systems for preventing fraud were 'clearly working':

> 716. Anybody who has sat through the case I have just tried and listened to evidence of electoral fraud that would disgrace a banana republic would find this statement surprising. To assert that 'The systems already in place to deal with the allegations of electoral fraud are clearly working' indicates a state not simply of complacency but of denial.

> 717. The systems to deal with fraud are not working well. They are not working badly. The fact is that there are no systems to deal realistically with fraud and there never have been. Until there are, fraud will continue unabated.

The second judgment was given in 2008 and is known as the 'Slough judgment'. Once again, Judge Mawrey found an electoral candidate and his associates guilty of corrupt and illegal practices and ordered a new election to be held. The candidate and some of his associates were subsequently the subject of criminal prosecutions and received substantial prison sentences at Reading Crown Court. The judge slated the authorities for a pusillanimous response to the possibilities for fraud identified in the first judgment.

In 2013 came the third case, concerning an election for a ward in Woking. In a judgment every bit as stinging as the previous two, Judge Mawrey stripped the electoral victory from the defendant and held that, once again, the election had been procured by corrupt practices. He noted:

> Reform of electoral registration has been promised for some time but, strangely enough, always mañana. The whole question of election law has been passed to the Law Commission for a thorough overhaul and consolidation. It is no criticism of the Law Commission to say that, with the best will in the world, its labours will not – indeed cannot – bear fruit until (if we are lucky) just before the 2020 General Election.

There is no need for hyperbole about the shambles involved in the three cases; gross abuse of the democratic system speaks for itself. It is hard to work out why there was such hopeless inaction on the part of the authorities. Plain incompetence could surely not be the whole explanation, though there was some evidence of it. The chief returning officer at the time of the election the subject of the Birmingham judgment, Lin Homer, was criticised by the judge for 'throwing the rule book out the window' when dealing with postal voting. He cleared her of deliberate obstruction but ruled that she had presided over a 'corrupt and fraudulent' vote and had failed to follow the correct procedures.

The only other explanation offered for the abrogation of duty by all concerned was a fear of being accused of cultural insensitivity, given that the wrongdoers in all three cases were from a Pakistani Muslim background. In November 2013, the Attorney General, Dominic Grieve QC, said that there was a problem of corruption in that particular minority community.[5] Despite adding various qualifications, he came in for immediate criticism and in short order withdrew his comments and apologised.

If it is true that the authorities were paralysed by such fears, there are four straightforward responses. First, it has to be possible to identify a problem in a particular community without being silenced. For example, the football hooliganism which blighted Britain in the 1980s was overwhelmingly a problem in the white working class community, and no one would have profited from denying it. Secondly, a failure to act would be less supportive and more of an affront to the majority of the community in question, whom it can safely be assumed would not want to be held to lower standards than everyone else. Thirdly, the fraud carried out in each of the three cases could easily have been done by any other community (and Judge Mawrey expressly said that it could and probably had been), and the measures needed to prevent it (cleaning up, or better still abandoning, postal voting) could all be done without any culturally-specific action. Finally, a failure to act would play into the hands of racially prejudiced individuals who would claim that there had been a conspiracy or unjust favouritism

---

[5] 'Corruption rife in the Pakistani community, says minister', *Telegraph*, 22 November 2013, http://www.telegraph.co.uk/news/politics/10469448/Corruption-rife-in-the-Pakistani-community-says-minister.html.

towards particular minorities. Far from lessening community tensions, therefore, ignoring fraud would in the long run only exacerbate them.

Afterword

At long last the Electoral Commission seemed to wake up to its responsibilities. In 2012 it published a report on electoral fraud,[6] and in 2015 it published research which it had commissioned following Judge Mawrey's judgments (albeit very belatedly).[7] But it came too late for the London Borough of Tower Hamlets, where another debacle took place in 2015, which resulted in the removal by the electoral court of the Mayor, Lutfur Rahman. Judge Mawrey QC was again the judge. He did not pull his punches, saying that Rahman had 'driven a coach and horses' through local authority law and had 'engaged in corrupt and illegal practices' to win elections. He concluded with these forthright words:[8]

> 685. On past form, it appears inevitable that Mr Rahman will denounce this judgment as yet another example of the racism and Islamophobia that have hounded him throughout his political life. It is nothing of the sort. Mr Rahman has made a successful career by ignoring or flouting the law (as this Petition demonstrates) and has relied on silencing his critics by accusations of racism and Islamophobia. But his critics have not been silenced and neither has this court.

> 686 Events of recent months in contexts very different from electoral malpractice have starkly demonstrated what happens when those in authority are afraid to confront wrongdoing for fear of allegations of racism and Islamophobia. Even in the multicultural society which is 21st century Britain, the law must be applied fairly and equally to everyone. Otherwise we are lost.

[6] http://www.electoralcommission.org.uk/__data/assets/pdf_file/0008/164609/Electoral-fraud-review-final-report.pdf.

[7] http://www.electoralcommission.org.uk/__data/assets/pdf_file/0003/181254/Elections-voting-and-election-fraud-Jan-2015.pdf.

[8] *Erlam and others v Rahman and others*. The judgment can be found online at http://news.bbc.co.uk/1/shared/bsp/hi/pdfs/judgment.pdf (Retrieved 25 April 2015).

Part IX: Sport and the Law

INTRODUCTION

Once upon a time, sport was considered more or less a private activity, wholly outside the law's jurisdiction. The state had no involvement in running or regulating sporting fixtures, large or small. Except it was never quite as simple as that, and it certainly is not the case now. As far back as Edward III, foolish time-wasting games were outlawed by statute because they interfered with archery practice. Seventeenth-century Puritans famously did not like games of any sort. After the Puritans, gambling became a major problem in sport, at least from the 18th century, where one can find statutes trying to stop or regulate it. One could go on.[1]

The first case in this part concerns an important player from the early days of West Indian cricket, Learie Constantine, who went on to become an important player in the early days of English anti-discrimination law. It is unlikely the circumstances giving rise to the case would have happened had Constantine not been a well-known and highly regarded sportsman, and one retains a residual suspicion that the case may not have been decided in the same way either.

Next we turn to a leading player from a different sport, the soccer goalkeeper Bruce Grobbelaar. Grobbelaar sued to protect his own reputation from being smeared by the most severe of sporting blights, the allegation that he had been involved in illegal match-fixing. His victory, as will be seen, was rendered hollow by the derisory award of damages he obtained, and in that respect was an illustration of the common law finding a practical solution to a technical problem: Grobbelaar, as the courts held, had brought the whole thing upon himself, and was made to pay the price.

The final essay considers two more discrimination cases from the world of cricket, one with rather more seriousness than

---

[1] I have, at some greater length, in *Court and Bowled*, Chapter 1.

the other. The serious case concerned whether an umpire might be elbowed out by a fixed retirement age. Needless to say, that issue has a much wider application than the sporting context in which it arose. The less serious case concerned someone falling over themselves to try and preserve the appearance of umpiring impartiality. I suppose one might call the case a joke gone too far.

No Room at the Inn

Sir Learie Constantine, sometime High Commissioner for Trinidad and Tobago, sometime clerk, sometime professional cricketer, barrister-at-law, politician, and at all times active and honoured campaigner against racial hatreds; how impossible to sum him up in a phrase. May it perhaps be sufficient to note that it has just been possible to compare him, almost in the same breath, with Ariel and with Falstaff? Of how many cricketers could I do this and live? Let him warm his hands at that, too.

Ronald Mason, *Sing All A Green Willow*[2]

One of the best known discrimination cases in Britain in recent years concerned the proprietors of a B&B wanting to impose conditions on the rooms they were prepared to let to guests. In *Bull v Hall*,[3] the Supreme Court eventually ruled that the proprietors were not permitted lawfully to refuse to let a room with a double bed to a same-sex couple, despite the proprietors' sincerely-held religious beliefs about marriage. The ruling was not without controversy, but it was certainly not disputed that as a general proposition people should not be discriminated against on the basis of arbitrary factors such as gender, orientation or race.

Seven decades ago, however, things were rather different. None of the modern legal weapons against such discrimination existed. Thus, when the famous cricketer Learie Constantine was turned away from a hotel during the Second World War for no reason other than the colour of his skin, his remedies at law were much more limited. But he went on to win an important High Court victory nonetheless, establishing an important step in the development of modern anti-discrimination law.

---

[2] Epworth Press, 1967, p 51. Note that Mason was writing before Constantine's ennoblement.

[3] [2013] UKSC 73. See *Cases that Changed Our Lives*, vol II, Chapter 17.

Constantine had been a respected cricketer before the war, even if his overall career statistics were not of the highest class (it was generally felt they did not reflect his ability or his contribution). He took West Indies' first ever test wicket, and is often said to have contributed to the development of a distinctive Caribbean style of play. His final test was in England just before the war. He remained in England during the conflict as a Ministry of Labour welfare officer assisting West Indian workers. He was based in Liverpool. In July 1943 he travelled to London to play in an exhibition match, and arranged to stay with his family at the Imperial Hotel near Russell Square.

Although Britain in those days still controlled an Empire often run on openly racial grounds, it practised no formal discrimination within its own shores. There was accordingly nothing to suggest that Constantine might be refused entry to a hotel on racial grounds – quite the contrary, they knew who he was and seemed happy to receive him. After just one night, however, the hotel asked him to move to an alternative establishment under the same ownership. Not only that, but the staff member concerned allegedly employed a word that was considered offensive even then.

The reason for that dismal turn of events was a new phenomenon in Britain, in the form of the American servicemen stationed there in advance of the invasion of Nazi-occupied Europe. Since the Civil War (in which several black units had fought for the North with distinction), segregation had so infected the US Army that some soldiers were actually given official warnings that in Britain they would have to expect to see black people being served in pubs and otherwise treated as equals. Clearly some did not accept the message, since it was their complaints, supinely acceded to by the hotel management, that led to the request for Constantine to leave.

Constantine did as he was asked, but then sought legal redress for his treatment. He did not bring an action in contract, possibly because the alternative accommodation offered meant few damages could have been recovered. Instead, he brought a tortious action based on old authorities which held that innkeepers could not refuse accommodation to travellers without 'lawful excuse'.

The action was tried in June 1944, in a bomb-proof courtroom (the second blitz was under way), less than two weeks after many of the offending American servicemen would have gone into action on D-Day. The defendants conceded that Constantine was a man of 'high character' and that they had had no reasonable ground on which to refuse him. But they pointed to the fact that they had given him alternative accommodation, and argued that he had therefore suffered no loss. Without proof of special damages, they submitted, Constantine had no cause of action.

The judge rejected that defence. Although there was no authority directly on point, he held that Constantine's action was founded on a right (to accommodation at a public inn absent a valid reason for refusal), which had been violated, and that the law would afford a remedy. He also held, however, that although Constantine had suffered 'much unjustifiable humiliation and distress', the authorities did not permit an award of special damages. Constantine therefore obtained judgment in his favour, but was only awarded nominal damages of five guineas.[4]

It might have been only a symbolic victory, but Constantine had obtained justice nonetheless. A major step towards outlawing discrimination had been taken, especially as public opinion was resoundingly in his favour over the case.

Constantine's cricketing career ended just after the war, finishing on a high note when he was unanimously voted by his (all white) teammates as captain of a Dominions XI to play England in a celebratory match in 1946. He then became a barrister and campaigner for civil rights. He served as High Commissioner for Trinidad, and played an important role in creating the Race Relations Act 1965. As his final milestone, in 1969 he became the first black member of the House of Lords, though his ill health prevented much involvement before his death in 1971.

---

[4]   See [1944] KB 693.

There seems little doubt that Constantine's status as an eminent cricketer greatly aided his case and showed the hotel's actions in a particularly poor light. His case therefore stands as a classic illustration of how cricket can go, in the words of one of its most famous historians, well beyond a boundary.[5]

[5] Published in the *New Law Journal*, 1 August 2014, vol 154, p 22.

Bribes and Dives

Liverpool dominated English football in the 1980s, winning six league titles, two European Cups, two FA Cups and four League Cups. It is therefore not hard to imagine the shock to all football fans – and for that matter beyond footballing circles – when in 1994 the *Sun* newspaper came across recordings of Bruce Grobbelaar, the club's star goalkeeper for most of that era, apparently agreeing to fix matches. The publication of the recordings and the inevitable litigation over them took an unexpected course, and raised some interesting questions for both sport and law.

Following the *Sun*'s revelations, Grobbelaar was charged with the criminal offence of conspiracy to corrupt. He pleaded not guilty. His defence was that he had only been obtaining evidence for the police, and had never intended actually to cheat. There were two trials, in which the jury failed to reach a verdict. Thereafter, Grobbelaar sought to clear his name completely by suing the *Sun* for libel. The *Sun* relied on the defence of justification, contending that it had been fully entitled to say what it had.

There was some dispute over what the *Sun* had implied by its articles, and thus what the 'sting' of the libel was. In turn that affected what the *Sun* had to prove by way of justification. Grobbelaar argued that the *Sun* had to prove not simply that he had entered into the corrupt agreements (which he did not deny) but also that he had actually let in goals deliberately. To prove that he had not done the latter he brought in expert evidence, in the form of the famous commentator and former goalkeeper Bob Wilson and the former keeper and manager Alan Ball. Both testified that Grobbelaar's performance in the matches in question was not consistent with anyone giving less than 100%. The *Sun* on the other hand argued that all it had to prove was that Grobbelaar had made corrupt agreements, whereupon his reputation would be destroyed irrespective of what had actually happened on the pitch.

The trial was held before a jury (libel actions are one of the very few non-criminal cases where jury trials can still take place). The burden of proof was on the *Sun*, but as the judge told the jury, the *Sun* did not have to prove each and every allegation. It simply had to prove 'the substantial truth of the message that Mr Grobbelaar dishonestly took bribes and fixed or attempted to fix matches'. Evidently it did not prove as much to the jury's satisfaction, for the result was a verdict for Grobbelaar and the substantial award of £94,000 in damages.

A stunned *Sun* appealed to the Court of Appeal. Had the case been a criminal one, and Grobbelaar acquitted by a jury, then no appeal could have been brought; Grobbelaar would have walked free. But both sides accepted that as the case was a civil one, the Court of Appeal did have jurisdiction to overturn verdicts that were 'perverse'. Moreover, once it was accepted that the Court of Appeal had the power to do so, it followed that it had a *duty* to do so in the appropriate circumstances.

And that is precisely what the Court of Appeal proceeded to do. It could not accept that the *Sun* had been anything other than fully justified in printing the accusations, based on the compelling evidence of corrupt agreements. The jury's verdict was therefore overturned and judgment entered in favour of the *Sun*. Grobbelaar, facing ruin, appealed to the House of Lords.[6]

The majority in the House of Lords took a somewhat more restrained view of the case. Lord Bingham observed that no jury could have thought anything other than that Grobbelaar had made corrupt agreements, based not just on the damning evidence of the tapes, but also inconsistencies in his evidence and his failure to report the agreements to the authorities, despite the bedrock of his defence being that he had made the agreements only to expose the corruption of others. But his lordship also pointed out that there was no evidence to rebut the testimony of Grobbelaar's distinguished witnesses that he had not actually thrown the matches in question.

The situation therefore was that Grobbelaar had entered into diabolical agreements with some corrupt individuals, but

---

[6] *Grobbelaar v News Group Newspapers Ltd and Another* [2002] UKHL 40.

had nevertheless given his all on the pitch in breach of those agreements. The *Sun* had been right about the former but not the latter. So what was a fair result? The House of Lords decided on a pragmatic solution. Grobbelaar was entitled to say he had been libelled. But the essence of libel was (and is) the protection of reputation. Having accepted that he made the corrupt bargains, and having failed to alert the authorities as he should have done, Grobbelaar's reputation was worthless. He was entitled to damages, but only of the minimum sum of £1. He was also ordered to pay the *Sun*'s legal costs.

The result was a financial disaster for Grobbelaar, who was declared bankrupt not long afterwards, but the limited victory he achieved meant he was able to keep playing professionally. It also seems to have preserved his reputation with at least a portion of the Anfield faithful. He played for the club in an exhibition match in 2006 and was also voted second best goalkeeper in Liverpool's history in a poll the same year. The *Sun*, for its part, was at the time of writing the second most popular daily in the United Kingdom, so its reputation was certainly not adversely affected.

Of far greater importance than the personal fortunes of the protagonists, needless to say, is the present state of match fixing in professional football. Lacking information and expertise on the subject, however, I shall refrain from speculation.[7]

---

[7] I have written in much more detail about cricket corruption: see *Court and Bowled*, p 182ff, but the very different nature of football means there is probably not much overlap between the two games.

The Umpire's Lot

Two press stories from 2014 showed that the lot of a cricket umpire is not always a happy one off the field, any more than it can be on it. Two respected umpires of many years standing were told they were too old to continue, while another faced the unusual charge that he was too Church of England. Both propositions would have satirists reaching for their keyboards, but in both cases there was a serious legal issue that had much wider implications than the foibles of flannelled fools in whites.

According to *The Times*,[8] the umpires Peter Willey (an iron-willed batsman for England a few years ago, and the subject of two of the better known commentary anecdotes[9]) and George Sharp wished to bring a complaint against the England and Wales Cricket Board (ECB) in the employment tribunal, alleging age discrimination. Both Willey and Sharp were about to reach 65 years of age, and under the ECB rules both faced compulsory retirement accordingly. They seemed to have at least an arguable case: from 2011, mandatory retirement at 65 was no longer automatically legally defensible. Instead, employers were required to show an 'objective justification'.

The role of an umpire requires an extensive knowledge of cricket, together with the ability to deal with at least mildly stressful situations. If anything, both qualities are likely to be enhanced by age. On the other hand, umpiring also requires stamina, concentration, sharp eyesight and acute hearing, and it is not being ageist to observe that all of those abilities erode with time (and that erosion comes to us all). Cricketing history has more than a few tales of once-respected umpires stubbornly carrying on well beyond the point where their senses had dulled

---

[8]   28 August 2014.

[9]   On one occasion, when he was facing the feared Jamaican fast bowler Michael Holding, the commentator Brian Johnson supposedly deadpanned 'The bowler's Holding, the batsman's Willey'; his *bon mot* must be the most oft-cited cricket quote in the past forty years. Some way behind is the scorecard when Willey caught an equally feared Australian fast bowler off the English bowler Graham Dilley: 'Lillee caught Willey bowled Dilley' read the relevant entry.

too far, yet apparently remaining unsackable because of their earlier reputation or because of ineffective officialdom.

Then again, all individuals age at different rates, and different jobs require different skills, some of which will decline quicker than others. Both those considerations suggest a fixed figure is inappropriate for determining retiring ages across all spheres of employment.

The only problem with a more flexible approach is that it leaves room for argument (and ultimately litigation) in individual cases, with the resultant expense and uncertainty. Yet even if one decides, for reasons of certainty, that a fixed age for retirement (and collection of superannuation) is appropriate, the long-standing figure of 65 might need to be revised in light of substantially improved living standards. The average life expectancy has increased markedly in the past few decades, and a person of 75 today might well be just as fit and capable as the average 65-year-old 50 years ago, albeit perhaps not for labour-intensive jobs. (Whether one agrees or not, the parlous state of our public finances might soon require the raising of the pensionable age out of economic necessity.) It follows that Willey and Sharp had a reasonable prospect of success. The *Daily Telegraph*[10] reported:

> A councilor and cricket enthusiast has been told he cannot umpire a church match because of fears he may not be 'theologically neutral' as his great-great grandfather was a bishop.

> Michael Claughton, who has 18 years' experience as a cricket umpire, offered to officiate the match between the Church of England XI and Vatican XI, due to take place later this month.

> But he said he was left baffled after officials said he could not be considered for the charity because they wanted to ensure it was theologically 'neutral' and they feared his ancestry could make him biased against the Catholic team.

Assuming the report to be accurate, the officials' reasoning seems slightly odd – if one could trace Claughton's ancestry further back than Henry VIII, it would be a racing certainty that he would have Catholic forebears too. Moreover, I understand

---

[10]   7 September 2014.

both XI's share the same head office theologically, even if the branch management differs.

More seriously, natural justice requires that a judge recuse him or herself if there is any suggestion that he or she shares any form of relationship or common interest with the litigants. There have been some interesting disputes over the years as to whether a common religion between judge and litigant amounts to such a relationship, the answer probably being that it will do so only where the dispute actually involves the religion in some material respect, with the usual qualification about each case turning on its facts.

Secondly, what about social events such as Claughton's cricket match? Should the law bother getting involved? One might instinctively say it should not, but there have been occasions in which human rights fingers have been pointed accusingly towards a social event: a long-standing married couples' golf tournament was an early victim of human rights legislation in New Zealand, for example, when it was held to constitute unlawful discrimination on the basis of marriage. Then there were the private clubs which clung to their men-only membership policies until very recently (the Marylebone Cricket Club prominent among them).

Such questions would be more pertinent in Claughton's case if umpiring was his professional career and the game a remunerative fixture. As it stands, I assume that he would not be much affected by the slight. But the moral principle remains.

One of the match's organisers was reported as saying 'There's absolutely no question of Michael Claughton's skill as an umpire or his honesty. We just thought it would be a nice way of showing everybody this is neutral.' Well, I imagine it wasn't very nice for Claughton.

Afterword

Willey and Sharp lost their case before the employment tribunal, in early 2015.[11]

---

[11] See 'Peter Willey and George Sharp lose age discrimination case', *BBC Sport*, 13 March 2015, http://www.bbc.co.uk/sport/0/cricket/31878479.

Part X: Medico-legal cases

INTRODUCTION

Along with criminal and family law, medical law is one area of law guaranteed to attract public interest and the opinions of almost everyone. The subject ranges from some of the oldest questions of all – the duties of doctors with regard to their patients, for example, famously derives from Hippocrates in Ancient Greece – to cutting edge scientific advancements that were unheard of a generation ago and which have tended to catch the law on the hop as a result.

The first case in this section, concerning the Hillsborough victim Tony Bland, raises a mixture of the old and the new. The question of the right to life is as old as philosophy itself, no doubt. But, difficult though it might be to imagine, the issue of switching off life support for an adult had never been decided in English law before Bland's case was heard in the 1990s. The only precedent was found in cases involving babies with birth defects – and they revealed some attitudes and values that could most politely be described as outdated. The only explanation I can think of for the apparent legal novelty was that medical technology had previously not allowed for a similar situation; in earlier times, anyone brought to hospital in a similar condition to that of Bland would have been assessed as clinically dead and no attempt to prolong their life would have been made.

The second case, that of the conjoined twins known as 'Mary and Jodie', was headline news while it was being considered by the Court of Appeal at the turn of the century. One of the judges involved, Lord Justice Ward, said that half the population would agree with the result in the case and the other half would think the judges mad. I suspect otherwise: most people would think, on utilitarian grounds if nothing else, that the court made the correct decision, though that is not to deny that there were some arguments in the other direction. The case concerned a medical form of 'Sophie's Choice': whether to separate the twins and cause the certain and near-immediate death of one, or whether to decline to operate, with the inevitable consequence that both would die within a few months.

Finally in this part is a case involving an off-duty doctor who feared she might have caught a virus when trying to revive a dying person she had come across on her way home. The question was whether or not she should be entitled to have samples taken from the deceased's body, with or without consent of the deceased's family. It is once again a utilitarian view, but I would have no hesitation in saying that the rights of the doctor (the fact of her being a doctor is irrelevant to the outcome; any good Samaritan might have attempted the same thing) should have overridden the sensitivities of the family of the deceased.

A Right to Die

On 15 April 1989, Tony Bland, an 18-year-old football fan, travelled to watch his beloved Liverpool play an FA Cup semi-final fixture against Nottingham Forest. Soon after his arrival, serious problems developed with access to the ground. A crush formed at the outer gates. With the situation becoming desperate, the police decided to let the Liverpool fans in by a side gate, but left the tunnel access open. Thousands including Tony Bland poured down into already overcrowded pens where they had nowhere to move and could not escape the resultant deadly crush. The worst stadium disaster in British history rapidly unfolded. It has always been known by the name of the venue: the Hillsborough disaster.

The toll on the day itself was 94 injured and 768 wounded. At the time Tony Bland was one of the latter, having suffered crushed ribs and two punctured lungs. Those injuries interrupted the supply of oxygen in his brain, inflicting severe brain damage and leaving him in a persistent vegetative state (PVS).

A number of attempts to stimulate Bland were made by his family and doctors without success. Scans revealed no cortical activity in the brain, although the brain stem remained intact. The sad conclusion of all his family and carers was that he had no hope of recovery. In other words, Anthony Bland's body might have survived but Tony Bland the person was gone. His body remained alive only by artificial nutrition and hydration, and it required continuous care.

The question therefore arose as to whether Bland's treatment could and should be withdrawn, with the inevitable result of almost immediate death. He had left no 'living will' or otherwise recorded what he would have preferred to happen in such circumstances, though his father was later to testify that he was sure his son would never have wanted to live as a PVS patient.

The problem was that, given that Bland was still legally alive, any such move would on its face constitute murder. The legal position was that those caring for him owed him a legal duty to keep him alive and failure to discharge that duty was, at law, murder. At that time, the only indications at law where incapable patients were permitted to die by the withdrawal of treatment had concerned newborn babies, such as *Re C (a minor) (wardship: medical treatment)*;[1] *Re B (a minor)*[2] and *Re J (a minor) (wardship: medical treatment)*.[3] And in the earlier case of *R v Arthur*,[4] a doctor had been charged with attempted murder after a baby with Down's Syndrome had died after receiving nursing care only, the parents having rejected it (incidentally, the case looks extraordinarily dated in the attitude of all concerned to people with Down's Syndrome).

Bland's supervising doctor, a professional with some experience of PVS, received legal advice based on those earlier cases. The advice confirmed that if he were to follow the course of withdrawing treatment, he would indeed face a murder charge. His employer, the Airedale NHS Trust, therefore applied to the courts seeking declarations that they might lawfully discontinue all life-sustaining treatment and medical support measures, including ventilation, nutrition and hydration by artificial means; that any subsequent treatment given should be for the sole purpose of enabling him to end his life in dignity and free from pain and suffering; that if death should then occur, its cause should be attributed to the natural and other causes of his present state; and that none of those concerned should, as a result, be subject to any criminal or civil liability.

The High Court granted the declaration, though not in all of the terms sought. It held that withdrawing treatment was in Bland's best interest and consistent with good medical practice. On behalf of Bland, the Official Solicitor appealed.

By this time the case had attracted considerable publicity. This was partly due to the legal novelty, since as we have seen all previous cases of withdrawing treatment had concerned newborn babies who had suffered from severe defects, rather than adults like Bland who had had a tragic accident. No doubt

[1]   [1989] 2 All ER 782.
[2]   [1990] 3 All ER 927.
[3]   [1990] 3 All ER 930.
[4]   (1981) 12 BMLR 1.

the publicity also followed in part from the ongoing public interest in the aftermath of Hillsborough.

Evidence was given by a number of eminent medical practitioners, including Professor Bryan Jennett, one of the two experts who had devised the phrase 'PVS' many years earlier. The opinion of experts on all sides was that Bland had no awareness and could experience no pain or pleasure, and there was no hope of any recovery.

In those circumstances, the Court of Appeal affirmed the decision of the High Court. The Official Solicitor appealed to the House of Lords.

All five law lords who heard the appeal gave a reasoned judgment of their own, and as with the Court of Appeal they unanimously dismissed the appeal.[5] All agreed that, although the object of medical treatment and care was to benefit the patient, since a large body of informed and responsible medical opinion was of the view that existence in a PVS state was of no benefit to the patient, the principle of the sanctity of life, which was not absolute, would not be violated by ceasing to give medical treatment. The care needed to keep Bland alive involved invasive manipulation of his body, to which he had not consented and from which he did not benefit.

It followed that Dr Howe and his colleagues were not under a duty (and according to Lord Browne-Wilkinson were not even entitled) to continue the care. The time had come when Bland had no further interest in being kept alive and there was no justification for the invasive care and treatment. Therefore, in legal terms, the omission to perform what had previously been a duty (keeping a patient alive by invasive treatment) would no longer be unlawful.

Shortly thereafter palliative care was withdrawn and Tony Bland became the 96th person to die from the Hillsborough

---

[5] *Airedale NHS Trust v Bland* [1993] 1 All ER 821. I have written elsewhere about the tendency for appellate courts to give multiple judgments, and the problems that arise from the practice: see James Wilson and Alexander Horne, 'Judgment Matters', *New Law Journal*, vol 160, 17 December 2010.

tragedy (one of the other injured having predeceased him), making the final toll 96 dead and 766 injured.

The decision seems manifestly correct, despite due regard to the tragic circumstances and the necessarily very great caution that any form of withdrawal of medical treatment must entail. I for one would never wish to live as a PVS patient, nor would I wish that on anyone I know. But it is right to record some of the strong objections that others have raised. Broadly speaking these fall into two categories. First, some argue, often (though not exclusively) on religious grounds, that all human life should be treated as sacred and inviolate and that doctors should remain under a duty to preserve life even in its most reduced form.

This places us in deep philosophical waters, where logic may not have the last word. Voluminous texts have been written on the subject, which for space reasons apart from anything else we cannot begin to discuss here. Ultimately, the question is whether it is more cruel than kind to keep alive someone whose cognitive function has disappeared entirely. There is a more difficult argument where a person is in agony, as with degenerative illnesses, and wishes to end his or her life whilst still in control of his or her mental faculties, as with the well-known cases of assisted suicide. In such cases it cannot be said that the person is to all intents and purposes is no longer there: quite the contrary, they may be not only conscious but with all their mental faculties intact. That dilemma is more appropriately described as 'whose life is it anyway?': should a person be entitled to make their own judgment about their own life, or must it always remain the case that where there is life there is hope? The fear is that a person might be coerced by greedy or uncaring family members, or unscrupulous doctors wanting to make hospital beds available for more deserving patients as they see it. Or it might be that a patient underestimates the value of their life as perceived by their family and friends.

Those considerations do not arise, however, in cases such as *Bland* where all agreed that the person that he was had ceased to exist.

The second objection to the *Bland* decision is the 'floodgates' or 'slippery slope' argument: that if one person is allowed to die by having treatment withdrawn, then many more may follow – including, perhaps, those where the question of surviving cognitive function is not so clear cut. Again, this is a familiar argument with regard to euthanasia and assisted suicide.

In response I would argue that, short of anarchy, we are always on the slippery slope with regulation: if we ban or allow *x*, then we are on the road to proscribing or permitting *y*. With the right safeguards in place injustice should not be inevitable. In cases such as Bland's the safeguards would be (and in fact are) along the lines of requiring a minimum number of doctors to undertake independent assessments and agree that withdrawal of treatment is appropriate; for the Official Solicitor to review the decision on behalf of the patient; and for an appeal procedure or, at the last, judicial review, to be available to challenge any decision if there is a serious dispute.

In the years since, a number of other cases have followed which have further refined the circumstances in which treatment of PVS or the terminally ill might be withdrawn. Almost 30 cases at the time of writing have been reported in the higher courts which have referred to *Bland*.[6] They have further explained the circumstances under which treatment may be withdrawn, though the basic principle and holdings in *Bland's* case remain good law.

No one would claim that any system can be perfect, but one does not need to resort to cliché to point out that perfection when dealing with extreme cases of human suffering is almost by definition unobtainable. The law lords in *Bland's* case reached the correct decision, in a case involving the most tragic circumstances.[7]

---

[6] There are also relevant cases from overseas, for example: the Canadian case of *Nancy B v Hôtel-Dieu de Québec* (1992) 86 DLR (4th) 385, which concerned a patient with Guillain-Barré syndrome. It was the opposite of Bland's case, in that she had all her mental faculties but could not breathe and depended for continued life on a ventilator. The New Zealand case of *Auckland Area Health Board v A-G* [1993] 1 NZLR 235 concerned a patient in a more advanced state of that syndrome, whose brain was alive but incapable of controlling the body because the conductivity of the nervous system had been destroyed.

[7] Published in *Criminal Law & Justice Weekly*, vol 177, 23 March 2013, p 198.

A Right to Live

At the turn of the century, the courts were presented with a case which gave rise to an ethical dilemma of the starkest and cruelest form; no less tragic than that of Tony Bland a few years earlier.[8] It concerned conjoined twins, referred to as 'Mary and Jodie', whose parents and carers faced what might be called 'Sophie's Choice' in relation to their lives.

The parents were from Gozo, an island near Malta, but the twins were born in the United Kingdom (pursuant to an historic agreement between the respective countries). Tragically, it was found that the twins could not survive in their conjoined condition, but only Jodie could survive independently, because she alone had normal organs capable of supplying oxygenated blood. Mary was alive because there was a common artery from which she was receiving Jodie's blood. Jodie could not continue supplying the blood for long; the evidence was that her heart would give out within three to six months. Therefore, unless she was separated from Mary, both would die. If they were separated, Jodie could expect a relatively normal life expectancy. Mary, on the other hand, would die almost immediately.

At this point, with due deference to competing arguments and emotions, it might be said that the case had an intuitive moral answer. To lose Mary would obviously be a tragedy, but the only alternative would be to lose both girls, which most people would consider even worse. But the parents did not see it that way. Guided by their devout Roman Catholic beliefs, they asserted that it was God's will that the children were afflicted as they were and that they had to be left in God's hands. The hospital therefore issued proceedings, seeking a declaration from the court that they should undertake the operation.

---

[8] *Re A (children) (conjoined twins: surgical separation)* [2000] 4 All ER 961. The full text can be found at http://www.bailii.org/ew/cases/EWCA/Civ/2000/254.html (Retrieved 31 January 2015). Note that Bailii has assigned the neutral citation [2000] EWCA Civ 254, but this would not have been the official citation from the court, because the practice of neutral citations did not begin until the following year.

The High Court held that the operation would enable Jodie to lead a relatively normal life; that the remaining months of Mary's life would be worthless to her and would also be hurtful; that to prolong her life for those few months would be seriously to her disadvantage; and therefore the operation would be in the best interests of both children. Moreover, it held that the operation was not to be regarded as a positive act, but as the withdrawal of Mary's blood supply, analogous to the situation where the court orders (as it did in Tony Bland's case) the withdrawal of food and hydration. Therefore, the operation would be lawful. The parents appealed.

In appropriately thorough and sensitive judgments, the Court of Appeal agreed unanimously to dismiss the appeal. No short summary can do the case justice, so all that is offered here is a short outline coupled with what I think was the key to the decision.

Lord Justice Ward was keen to stress at the outset both the unique facts of the case and that there would never be unanimous agreement by the general public over the outcome. He also emphasised that it was not a moral or ethical outcome that the court was required to find, but rather a legal answer – which might or might not coincide with the former.

There was no ready legal answer, because the facts were unprecedented. But that did not mean analogies could not be found with previous cases and other legal sources such as international agreements and domestic statutes. Given the international conventions (including, but not limited to, the European Convention on Human Rights) protecting the 'right to life', it was impermissible to deny that every life had an equal inherent value. Life was worthwhile in itself, whatever the diminution in a person's capacity to enjoy it, and however gravely a person's brain and other functions were impaired. Further, it was wrong to regard the proposed operation as an omission, rather than an action. It was not the same as withdrawing food or hydration. It was an invasion of Mary's bodily integrity, which would constitute an assault unless she consented (which she could not) or approval of the court was given.

Nevertheless, the court went on to approve the operation. The key to the legal justification was the following: Mary was, at law, not entitled to Jodie's blood supply, all the more so because it was killing both of them. In effect, she was – wholly unintentionally – committing an ongoing assault on Jodie by taking her blood. Thus, the doctors were entitled to intervene to ensure the cessation of that assault – to defend Jodie, in other words. The result would be Mary's tragic death, but it was the lesser of two evils.

I leave the last word to Ward LJ:

> Lest it be thought that this decision could become authority for wider propositions, such as that a doctor, once he has determined that a patient cannot survive, can kill the patient, it is important to restate the unique circumstances for which this case is authority. They are that it must be impossible to preserve the life of X. without bringing about the death of Y., that Y. by his or her very continued existence will inevitably bring about the death of X. within a short period of time, and that X. is capable of living an independent life but Y. is incapable under any circumstances (including all forms of medical intervention) of viable independent existence. As I said at the beginning of this judgment, this is a very unique case.

A Right to Know

Modern medical ethics have their origin in the very roots of Western Civilisation. There is the Hippocratic oath, deriving from the late fifth century BC. Then there is the Biblical Parable of the *Good Samaritan* (Luke 10:29–37), in which Jesus tells the story of the beaten and injured traveller (who might have been Jewish) by the side of the road, whom the Samaritan went out of his way to assist, despite the historic conflict between Jews and Samaritans. The resultant concept of 'neighbour' has been heavily influential not only in medical ethics but also in law, most famously in Lord Atkin's speech in *Donoghue v Stevenson*, as seen earlier in this book.

Fully imbued with modern ethics and the spirit of both Hippocrates and Luke was the claimant in the case of *CM v EJ*,[9] an interesting action raising some fundamental principles of medical law.

The claimant, referred to as 'CM', was a consultant and professor at one of London's principal teaching hospitals. In May 2013, she was driving home, off duty, when she saw a person, EJ, lying motionless on the pavement. EJ was seriously injured and had bled profusely. CM performed emergency first aid on EJ but the latter died at the scene. In the course of her resuscitative efforts, CM's hands became covered with EJ's blood.

CM noticed also that she had a number of abrasions on her hands, probably caused by the alcoholic handwash which she used in her work. She was anxious about the risk of being infected with a blood-borne disease and commenced a course of antiretroviral medication. The drugs left her feeling extremely unwell and had the potential for long-term health damage as well.

Naturally CM was anxious to establish as soon as possible whether she might have caught any serious illnesses. She therefore wanted samples of EJ's blood or tissue taken. The

---

[9]   [2013] EWHC 1680 (Fam).

coroner had no objection, but the problem was that he had no free-standing power to permit the sampling or testing. It had to come either from EJ's immediate living relatives, or from an order of the High Court.

The police were able to trace a quite remote family member, OP. He confirmed that EJ's parents lived abroad and were not yet aware of her death. OP stated that he was EJ's closest relative in the United Kingdom and gave his consent to the taking of a blood sample. But, to be on the legal safe side, CM issued proceedings in the High Court seeking declarations regarding the lawfulness of the sampling and testing.

The governing legislation was the Human Tissue Act 2004. It created a range of offences for removing, storing or using human tissue for purposes without appropriate consent. Under the 2004 Act, the Human Tissue Authority (HTA) was established to regulate activities concerning the removal, storage, use and disposal of human tissue; the HTA had in turn published Codes of Good Practice which were relevant to CM's application.

The judge in the High Court, Cobb J, held that 'consent' was the fundamental principle of the Act and the associated Codes. Consent underpinned the lawful removal, storage and use of body parts, organs and tissue. In particular, the Act provided that consent was required for material (such as blood or human tissue) to be removed, stored or used for 'obtaining scientific or medical information, which may be relevant to a person including a future person.' In the absence of the requisite consent, the removal, testing, or storing of human tissue would be a criminal offence (s 5).

The effect was that:

(i) A coroner could remove, store and use relevant material for the purpose of the post mortem examination to determine the cause of death without obtaining the consent of relatives;

(ii) A coroner did not have the power to consent to samples being taken for the benefit of a third party;

(iii) A coroner's consent was required before any sample could be removed, stored or used for purposes other than in the exercise of his own functions or authority.

In the circumstances, the judge held that it was 'not reasonably practicable' to seek the consents of EJ's parents for the removal or use of blood or tissue from EJ 'within the time available' (s 27(8)). There was no indication that EJ had other relatives in the list of 'qualifying' persons available from whom consent could be taken. Further, OP was a person in a 'qualifying relationship' within the definition of s 3(6)(c) and s 27(4)(h), for the purposes of giving consent to the removal, storage and use of samples of EJ's blood or human tissue. He had given relevant consent for the purposes of the Act. Furthermore, the coroner had indicated his agreement to the removal and testing of the relevant material, subject to the consent obtained from the qualifying person. Accordingly, that opened the gateway for the exercise of the court's discretion under the inherent jurisdiction to authorise the removal, storage and use of EJ's human tissue samples as sought by CM.

The jurisdictional hurdle crossed, the court had little hesitation in granting the relief sought. CM's request only arose because she had undertaken an act of great humanity in attempting to save EJ's life. If testing were not to be undertaken, CM would live for the foreseeable future in a state of profoundly anxious uncertainty as to whether she had contracted a serious, life-threatening illness. That would doubtless affect not only her personal wellbeing, but also her ability to treat other patients in the context of her highly skilled profession. Further, CM was suffering the harmful (and extremely discomforting) side effects of the antiretroviral medication.

CM's application was therefore allowed and the tests undertaken. Fortunately, the test results came back negative and CM was able to stop taking the antiretroviral drugs.

The result seems obvious in logic: no one could argue that CM should have been told as soon as possible if her act of spontaneous humanity had had tragic consequences. Unlike many other cases in this book, the facts were not unusual or improbable – anyone who incurs a cut in the course of helping another might be in the same situation.

Two interesting points remain. First, to what extent should a family's right to the body of a deceased be balanced against either the right of an individual such as CM to discover vitally important information? Suppose the family had refused consent, and CM had gone on to suffer unnecessary liver or kidney damage from the drugs?

As much as one's culture, religion or beliefs of any other sort deserve respect, EJ herself was dead and therefore no longer in possession of any rights as such (and what if she would not have objected to testing but had never recorded her views in writing, but her family were of some devout persuasion and had different ideas?). It seems to me that the coroner should have the power to undertake the testing in any case similar to CM's, and if the family objected once they had been informed they could seek injunctive relief or sue for damages, assuming they could establish that the coroner's actions or intended actions were unlawful.

The same sort of question arises also in the context of organ donation: a utilitarian approach might even require organ donation as a matter of course, irrespective of the wishes of the deceased, their family or anyone else.

The second interesting point about the case concerns the fact that in English law, CM's actions were purely voluntary, in contrast with the position in most civil law countries. A post on the case on the *UK Human Rights Blog*[10] explains the difference:

> [M]ost civil law countries impose a positive duty to rescue, which means that if a person finds someone in need of medical help, he or she must take all reasonable steps to seek medical care and render best-effort first aid. A famous example of this was the investigation into the photographers at the scene of Lady Diana's fatal car accident: they were suspected of violation of the French law of 'non-assistance à personne en danger' (deliberately failing to provide assistance to a person in

[10]   R. English, 'The good Samaritan doctor and the Human Tissue', *UK Human Rights Blog*, 26 June 2013, http://www.ukhumanrightsblog. com/2013/06/26/the-good-samaritan-doctor-and-the-human-tissue-act/ (Retrieved 10 July 2013).

danger), which can be punished by up to 5 years imprisonment and a fine of up to 70,000 euros.

Some food for thought, but let us leave Pandora's box closed for now.

Part XI: Writs, Wits and Wags: Characters of the Courtroom

Introduction

This final section of the book concerns a handful of characters who have enriched the courtroom in some way or another over the years. Prominent among them is the now retired Lord Justice Ward, who appears in the first two cases in this part. Ward LJ was a favourite of everyone in the court system – barristers, solicitors, court staff and litigants – over the course of his distinguished career, for his engaging wit and wry turn of phrase. He was kindly towards all – or nearly all – who appeared in front of him, but that did not stop him from issuing razor-sharp putdowns when anyone deserved it. Nor did it stop him making fearless decisions in the most difficult of cases – such as the conjoined twins case considered in the medico-legal section earlier in the book.

The final essay began life as a review I wrote for the *New Law Journal* about a book of bad judges; those who became memorable like Ward LJ but, unlike Ward LJ, for all the wrong reasons. I hope that does not leave readers with the wrong impression; the good judges deserved more of the book and, fortunately, there were (and are) rather more of them.

Tugboats and Pettifoggery

If there is a judge in modern times whose wit deserves comparison with the likes of Mark Twain, it is undoubtedly the now retired Sir Alan Ward, for 18 years a stalwart of the Court of Appeal, Civil Division. So it was no surprise that in his penultimate judgment, delivered after his formal retirement, a quotation from Mr Twain (real name Samuel Langhorne Clemens) featured prominently and appropriately. The case, *Reeves v Northrop*,[1] concerned something with which the 19th-century American author would have been thoroughly engaged – a wayfaring life aboard a houseboat. Unfortunately, it also featured two rather less engaging things which modern day English lawyers find tiresomely familiar, namely abysmally drafted legislation and pettifogging local authorities.

The case was brought by one Randy Northrop. He was a Californian in origin, but more of a wanderer in spirit. He moved to England in the late 1980s and purchased an old tugboat, the MY *Cannis*. He managed to convert the vessel into a houseboat, and lived on board with his family. After some time in Bristol they moved the *Cannis* to Chivenor in Devon. About two years later, they were featured in a local newspaper, which among other things explained that they did not pay council tax but neither did they receive various services such as electricity, water or rubbish collection.

Following the article's publication, readers offered a variety of responses. One correspondent suggested Northrop pay some council tax voluntarily 'and make [the council] acknowledge you have your right to live as you choose'. Northrop followed that advice – and there all his problems began. Instead of appreciating the gesture, the council responded with a statement banding the boat as 'Band A' as 'proof of being liable' and demanding that he pay the balance due for the two years in which he had been moored there at the time of the case.

[1] [2013] EWCA Civ 362.

Northrop challenged his liability in the valuation tribunal. Initially he represented himself. He began his written submissions with the quotation from Twain:

> Twenty years from now you will be more disappointed by the things you didn't do, than by the ones you did do. So throw off the bowlines. Sail away from the safe harbor, catch the trade winds in your sails. Explore. Dream. Discover.

Twain's sentiment also had some legal relevance, because the core of Northrop's challenge to council tax was that he did not intend to remain moored in the same place on a permanent basis. Moreover, the *Cannis* was not connected to any land services other than a hosepipe, and to reach it at high tide required a tender. Therefore, the *Cannis* did not constitute a dwelling of the sort that would otherwise attract the tax; or, in the arcane language of the applicable law, no rateable hereditament had been established.

The valuation tribunal accepted that argument, but the council appealed successfully to the High Court. One key point for the court was the length of time that the *Cannis* had been moored in the same place.

Northrop appealed in turn to the Court of Appeal. Sir Alan gave the leading judgment. After a genial introduction, in which he decided to refer to Northrop by his first name of Randy, he set about navigating through the distinctly choppy seas of the relevant legislation. There were seven sections to consider, found in four separate Acts of Parliament. After reviewing them all Sir Alan concluded:

> If prizes are to be offered for legislative gobbledegook then the foregoing would surely qualify. Having undertaken that trawl through these various statutes I confess to my shame I am no wiser nor would any ordinary citizen be without help from the Practice Note.

Which gives ample support to the various efforts that have been made over the year about tidying up the fairly tattered statute book.

Sir Alan then turned to the relevant case law, and concluded that the High Court had been correct: the *Cannis* was a permanent

206

fixture for the purposes of the legislation and accordingly Randy was liable for the tax.

Sir Alan finished with a nice rhetorical flourish:

> I am afraid, therefore, that Randy Northrop must lose and the appeal must be dismissed. I have a sneaking sympathy for him because he did not use many of the services which council tax is supposed to provide and it may have been harsh to list him in band A. But all of that is of no moment. He had indicated that he was soon to move and he has moved from the mooring. He has thrown off the bow lines and sailed away from the safe harbour though whether to catch the trade winds in his sails or just withstand the buffetings of the gales in the English Channel I know not. In as much as this is the penultimate judgment I shall write after 18 years in the Court of Appeal, I am a kindred spirit who has sailed away from the safe harbour of the Royal Courts of Justice, not at all sure how to explore, or what to dream or what I am about to discover.

Mark Twain famously said that Wagner's music was better than it sounds. Perhaps, in a similar vein, he might have thought that English law was better than it reads.[2]

---

[2] Published in the *New Law Journal*, vol 163, p 22, 8 November 2013.

Warding off Injustice

The retirement of Lord Justice Ward, whom we have just encountered, was a memorable occasion, funny and sad in equal measure. I particularly enjoyed an anecdote about the time he leant over the bench and told a litigant in person to 'get a life'. For offering that sage advice he was reprimanded by the judicial hierarchy, despite the fact that anyone who has experienced such individuals would agree with him. (Colonel Wintle was very much the exception to the rule.) Another litigant in person (associated with the *Fathers For Justice* campaign group) once appeared before him in full Darth Vader costume. Ward LJ politely asked him to remove his helmet and lightsaber, and proceeded to refer to him as 'Lord Vader' throughout the hearing.

One can imagine therefore Ward LJ's heart sinking when confronted by a case conducted by litigants in person on *both* sides.[3] He began his judgment with the following:

> [1] This judgment will make depressing reading. It concerns a dispute between two intelligent and not unsuccessful businessmen who, after years of successful collaboration, have fallen out with each other and this and other litigation has ensued with a vengeance. Being without or having run out of funds to pay for legal representation, they have become resolute litigators and they litigated in person. Some unlucky judge had to cope with the problems that inevitably arise in the management of a case like this. Here the short straw was drawn by His Honour Judge Anthony Thornton QC. He struggled manfully, patiently, politely, carefully and conscientiously. Many may not have done so. It is, therefore, hugely unfortunate that the appeal is launched essentially on the ground that the judge allowed himself to become distracted and so wrongly conducted the trial on the written information he had without allowing the defendants to call live evidence. The appeal is based upon that alleged procedural impropriety.

> [2] What I find so depressing is that the case highlights the difficulties increasingly encountered by the judiciary at all

---

[3] *Wright v Michael Wright Supplies Ltd* [2013] EWCA Civ 234.

levels when dealing with litigants in person. Two problems in particular are revealed. The first is how to bring order to the chaos which litigants in person invariably – and wholly understandably – manage to create in putting forward their claims and defences. Judges should not have to micro-manage cases, coaxing and cajoling the parties to focus on the issues that need to be resolved. Judge Thornton did a brilliant job in that regard yet, as this case shows, that can be disproportionately time-consuming. It may be saving the Legal Services Commission which no longer offers legal aid for this kind of litigation but saving expenditure in one public department in this instance simply increases it in the courts. The expense of three judges of the Court of Appeal dealing with this kind of appeal is enormous. The consequences by way of delay of other appeals which need to be heard are unquantifiable. The appeal would certainly never have occurred if the litigants had been represented. With more and more self-represented litigants, this problem is not going to go away. We may have to accept that we live in austere times, but as I come to the end of eighteen years' service in this court, I shall not refrain from expressing my conviction that justice will be ill served indeed by this emasculation of legal aid.

[3] My second concern is that the case shows it is not possible to shift intransigent parties off the trial track onto the parallel track of mediation. Both tracks are intended to meet the modern day demands of civil justice. The raison d'être (or do I simply mean excuse?) of the Ministry of Justice for withdrawing legal aid from swathes of litigation is that mediation is a proper alternative which should be tried and exhausted before finally resorting to a trial of the issues. I heartily agree with the aspiration and there are many judgments of mine saying so. But the rationale remains a pious hope when parties are unwilling even to try mediation. Judge Thornton attempted valiantly and persistently, time after time, to persuade these parties to put themselves in the hands of a skilled mediator, but they refused. What, if anything, can be done about that? You may be able to drag the horse (a mule offers a better metaphor) to water, but you cannot force the wretched animal to drink if it stubbornly resists. I suppose you can make it run around the litigation course so vigorously that in a muck sweat it will find the mediation trough more friendly and desirable. But none of that provides the real answer.

With which everyone who has experience of the court system would agree. Cutting legal aid to save costs carries the risk of becoming a classic example of false economy. It is not too much of an exaggeration to say that it is like the army deciding to save money by not hiring any field doctors, but instead to hand over medical supplies to soldiers and instructing them to do it themselves. Such an army might expect to have to spend more money on recruitment and training as a result.

There are five general observations I would make. First, it is generally necessary for litigants in person to be assisted with court procedure. Secondly, few have the skill of distilling relevant from irrelevant issues. Thirdly, even highly educated litigants in person are generally quite out of their depth in discussing any relevant authorities, statutes or points of principle, which therefore have to be explained at least to some extent (and even then the full significance is often not grasped). Fourthly, it is the duty of the other side's barrister to draw all relevant authorities to the court's attention and identify arguable points which the litigant might have missed, and this usually takes longer as the judge will want to be satisfied that that duty has been discharged. (It may also add to the (often unrecoverable) costs of the other side). Fifthly, judgments often take longer as the judges feel obliged to include more detail, with little homilies explaining points of law which ordinarily would not be necessary.

There is a more fundamental point, namely justice being done – and, equally, being seen to be done. If there is a basic inequality between representation of the parties, one is entitled to question whether the standard of the trial process will always be maintained. Law is a learned profession, as with, say, medicine or architecture, and it is idle to expect that a lay person could undertake even a straightforward medical diagnosis or design a simple building as well as a professional. It is equally expecting too much of lay people to assume they can competently represent themselves in court.

For a long time it was said that litigation could only be afforded in Britain by the very rich or the very poor. If the latter are denied legal aid then we will end up with another cliché, which has it that justice, like the Ritz, is open to all.

Afterword

Anyone doubting Sir Alan's wisdom should consider the case of *R (on the application of Salmon) v Feltham Magistrates' Court.*[4] The claimant litigant in person had just lost his case about council tax. The judge, Mr Justice Stadlen, then asked him if he wished to apply for permission to appeal to the Court of Appeal. (I interpolate that he might as well have asked an alcoholic if he would like his glass refilled, but duty required him to observe the formalities.) I often think that litigants in person act on the advice of the late Vivian Stanshall: 'be reasonable, ask for the impossible'.

The following exchange ensued:

The claimant: My papers just flipped open, it must have been an angel who came in and turned them over, on s 66 of the Local Government Finance Act . . . So we appear to have a problem because you actually yourself said there would be no ground on which the court could quash the order, the ground is unsustainable. Well, I am sorry, you have got every ground, according to that.

Stadlen J: Next.

The claimant: I think that it is clear and again on human rights grounds. I do not feel I have had a fair trial today. I do not actually feel that the interests of natural justice has been served.

Stadlen J: Why?

The claimant: Because there has been a total failure to really consider what I have been saying about ultra vires and it appears now, from what I have just discovered on s 66, that, you know, the basis – you based your judgment on para 57 of the regulations and they clearly contradict s 66(2)(b) of the Act, so again –

Stadlen J: You have not had a fair trial because I have not considered a matter that you have not drawn to my attention: is that your submission?

---

[4]   [2008] EWHC 3507 (Admin).

The claimant: You said there would be no ground on which this court could quash the order.

Stadlen J: Next?

The claimant: I think I have said enough.

Stadlen J: . . . I refuse leave . . . Anything else?

The claimant: I just feel I have to say that Jesus is waiting for you judges to see the light.

Mr Justice Stadlen: He is waiting for . . . ?

The claimant: Jesus is waiting for you judges to see the light.

Mr Justice Stadlen: Thank you very much.

Which if anything amounts to one of the less trying passages involving litigants in person that I have come across over the years.[5]

---

5   Published in the *New Law Journal*, vol 164, 4 July 2014, p 22.

Bad Judges

In *R v Sussex Justices; ex parte McCarthy*,[6] Lord Hewart LCJ famously said: '[I]t is not merely of some importance but is of fundamental importance, that justice should not only be done, but should manifestly and undoubtedly be seen to be done'

The aphorism found its way into the *Oxford Dictionary of Quotations*. Ironically, while it might be one of the greatest legal quotes of the 20th century, it was made by one of the very worst judges. In 1985, Lord Devlin wrote:[7]

> Hewart ... has been called the worst Chief Justice since Scroggs and Jeffries in the seventeenth century. I do not think that this is quite fair. When one considers the enormous improvement in judicial standards between the seventeenth and twentieth centuries, I should say that, comparatively speaking, he was the worst Chief Justice ever.

Many years later, Lord Hewart has found his way into Graeme Williams QC's *A Short Book of Bad Judges*, for reasons other than his famous quotation.

Williams explains that it occurred to him that whilst there were many biographies of great judges, there seemed to be almost nothing by way of books about bad ones, despite the fact that everyone who has had something to do with the law could, if they were honest, think of the odd example. Moreover, he argues, villains usually make for more entertaining characters. He offers *Paradise Lost* and *The Tales of Mr Toad* in contradistinction to *Paradise Regained* and *Flopsy Bunnies* by way of example.

In both respects he has a point. David Prowse correctly chose the villain ahead of the Wookie when offered a role in *Star Wars*. Sir Anthony Hopkins will probably be best remembered for Hannibal Lecter, out of more than a hundred film roles in his career. The model he used for Lecter's famously chilly voice was the even more menacing HAL, the antagonist supercomputer in

---

[6] [1924] 1 KB 256, 259. Incidentally, Lord Hewart presided over the appeal of William Wallace, whom we met in Chapter 5.
[7] *Easing the Passing: the Trial of Dr John Bodkin Adams.*

Kubrick's *2001: A Space Odyssey*, who was clearly the most important as well as the most memorable character in the film.

As to bad judges, I myself have come across an angry judge who continually embarrassed himself with his ill-tempered outbursts; an eminent QC who, upon elevation to the bench, repeatedly turned up to court late or ill-prepared; and, worst of all, a judge who had to be moved around different divisions of the High Court because almost everything he decided in his original position was overturned on appeal, virtually as a matter of routine.

Williams is therefore not ploughing fallow ground, even if, as he rightly says, the good judges far outweigh the bad ones across the centuries of the common law.

After an amusing introduction, quoting among others Francis Bacon (the Renaissance man, not the more recent artist), Williams offers ten examples of forgettable judicial officers. He starts with Lord Westerbury, who was forced out of his position as Lord Chancellor when a formal vote of censure was passed in Parliament against him for (among other things) a 'want of caution'. Mr Grayling take note.[8] Not that it ruined Westbury's career: he continued to sit as a judge.

Williams then considers two other 19th-century judges before introducing Lord Darling, whom he speculates might have been appointed to the Appellate Committee of the House of Lords by mistake – he should have been an ordinary peer, not a law lord. Darling's chief crime was what Bacon called

---

[8] At the time of writing, Chris Grayling was the Lord Chancellor. He had been a controversial appointment, given that he was the first holder of the post for centuries who had no legal background. Some even argued that his appointment was thereby void (see letters page of *The Times*, 7 September 2012). I do not think it was technically void, because the statute is so widely drafted. But I still objected to the appointment. Not only did Grayling lack the requisite expertise and standing in the profession, he was also an aspiring professional politician, reliant on his political party for career advancement. Lord Chancellors prior to the 2005 reform of the office had all been distinguished lawyers appointed straight from their legal careers (they were usually Queen's Counsels and thus senior barristers). Accordingly, they were unafraid of standing up for the rule of law and rocking the party boat where necessary, even though they were technically part of the Cabinet. Grayling was replaced after the 2015 election by another non-lawyer, Michael Gove.

a lack of gravity; for more modern readers he seems to have been something akin to the comedian Ricky Gervais's character David Brent: a comedian manqué whose court was full of 'guffawing idlers'.

Lord Hewart CJ's chapter makes for excruciating reading: a sorry tale of how he was appointed with no judicial experience and, as it turned out, no judicial ability.

Williams then discusses some other High Court judges, before showing some even-handedness by including bad circuit judges.

It is hard to argue with the choices for his judicial rogues' gallery. There will obviously be more marginal or controversial candidates. Lord Denning, for example, famously polarised opinion: some thought him a great social reformer and praised him for his gratifyingly clear prose. Others found him a tiresome maverick whose popularity was due mainly to his short sentences and simplistic reasoning. Lord Cooke of Thorndon, something of a spiritual successor to Lord Denning as a precedent-disregarding social reformer, divided opinion in a similar way, except he could never be accused of using short sentences.

Given that the purpose of the book is entertainment rather than education (though it provides a pleasing incidental contribution towards the latter), Williams was probably right to stick to the less controversial choices. His book will make for an enjoyable commuting companion, the only real complaint being that it is a too-short short book.

A few years ago I witnessed a very good judge cut a bombastic barrister down to size, as the latter passed up an old case:

Barrister: 'My lord, in these days, of course, 1899 judgments are extremely short and to the point'.

Judge: 'Are they neither now?'

Barrister: 'My lord, those were the days.'

Judge: 'I expect counsel were as well'.

In that spirit, perhaps a member of the judiciary might want to respond to Williams' short book of bad judges with a longer book of bad barristers ...[9]

---

[9] Review of *A Short Book of Bad Judges*, by Graeme Williams QC (Wildy, Simmonds & Hill, 2014). Published in the *New Law Journal*, 22 May 2014, p 22. Sadly, Mr Williams has since died.

Part XII: A Final Word

This book has given 50 examples of the law in action, over a time period exceeding a century, and involving characters as diverse as captains and colonels, playwrights and pianists, and purchasers of mundane consumer goods. I have tried to shed a bit of light on the background stories behind most of the cases, which aside from the intrinsic human interest can often add insights into why the law reached the decision it did.

I would expect – and hope – that readers will have different views about the merits of each decision, and disagree with at least some. But I hope the overall impression of the legal system is not wholly negative. I doubt the common law could have survived for as long as it has – and not just in England and Wales, but throughout the former Empire and even beyond that – if it was not fit for purpose. The amount of invisible exports made by the legal profession in London provides a tidy sum to the Treasury each year. In that respect, it should be noted that international litigants are a hard-nosed group not in the habit of spending money unwisely, least of all when their commercial reputation and livelihood is at stake.

So there must be something going for the common law. I once attended a speech by the Attorney-General of Qatar,[1] a highly educated and distinguished lawyer, needless to say, who offered an outsider's perspective. The common law, he said, was an achievement not just for England and Wales but for all of humanity: a system of justice that was fair and seen to be fair to everyone by everyone. That was a fairly ringing endorsement, and seems an appropriate note on which to finish this book.

James Wilson
Dulwich
May 2015

---

[1] I wrote a short report of the occasion: 'Qatar Law Forum, Mansion House, London 17 December 2012', *Halsbury's Law Exchange*, 25 January 2013, http://www.halsburyslawexchange.co.uk/qatar-law-forum-mansion-house-london-17-december-2012/ (Retrieved 3 March 2015).

Index